Paris
and other
Disappointments

Adam Rozenbachs is a stand-up comedian, writer, broadcaster, actor and voiceover artist. He has steadily risen to become one of Australia's funniest and most consistent performers, writers and broadcasters.

ADAM ROZENBACHS

Paris and other Disappointments

VIKING

an imprint of

PENGUIN BOOKS

VIKING

UK | USA | Canada | Ireland | Australia
India | New Zealand | South Africa | China

Penguin
Random House
Australia

Viking is part of the Penguin Random House group of companies
whose addresses can be found at global.penguinrandomhouse.com.

First published by Viking, 2019

Cover design by Alex Ross © Penguin Random House Australia Pty Ltd
Cover images courtesy Mark Weiss/Getty Images (snowglobe), Jamesmcq24/Getty Images
(Eiffel Tower), tadamichi/Shutterstock (puddle) and gopfaster/Shutterstock (shard)
Typeset in Adobe Caslon Pro by Midland Typesetters, Australia
Printed and bound in Australia by Griffin Press, part of Ovato, an accredited
ISO AS/NZS 14001 Environmental Management Systems printer.

A catalogue record for this
book is available from the
National Library of Australia

ISBN 978 0 14379 339 7

penguin.com.au

For anyone who's ever had a parent

MELBOURNE

The reason I agreed to travel to Europe with my dad was because I was sick of having fun overseas. Enjoying myself, meeting exciting people, learning about other cultures – all things I could do without.

The seven innocuous words that started our journey were, 'I'd bloody love to go to Europe.' Dad had been repeating them at family gatherings for years, often after I'd recounted a recent holiday I'd been on.

Usually these words were just taken as conversation filler, like Dad bemoaning not signing us up as MCC members at birth, but this time I decided to take them seriously. To be honest, I reacted before I'd properly thought it through – the way someone might instinctively pull a child to safety, or grab a hot sausage straight off the barbecue and throw it in their mouth, burning all available skin. I said to Dad, 'Well, let's go then.'

If he wanted to go, why not? I was single, I didn't have kids and I was a television writer and comedian; big chunks of time off were part of my landscape. And for once, I didn't already have a holiday booked. The timing couldn't have been better.

And if I didn't get proactive, soon we'd reach a point where Dad could no longer go. Then every family gathering until death would be him lamenting, 'I wish I'd bloody gone to Europe.'

'I'm serious, Tommy,' I said. 'I finish at the end of September and don't have to be back at work until November. If you really want to go, I can do it.'

Dad was speechless; he hadn't expected that. His bluff had been called. He wasn't the only one who was stunned – I'd never considered it for a second before, yet suddenly I was all-in on a European trip with him.

Agreeing so hastily had the feeling of making drunken plans late on a big night, except that this plan wouldn't be forgotten in a hungover haze the next morning, because we were sober. And there were witnesses. Dad and I both knew it would be an extraordinary act to back out from there. It was also impossible because I get my stubbornness from him, so neither of us would have known how to retreat, even if we'd wanted to.

Besides, no one but me was in a position to take Dad to Europe. Mum was never going to do a big trip; she gets nervous enough watching *Getaway*. My sister, Michelle, still lived at home, so she already had her daily fill of Dad. My older brother, Jason, couldn't do it because he was no longer with us; he lives in Research, an outer Melbourne suburb, so no one's going to give him a lift to the airport.

I'm not from a family of travellers. Mum and Dad both immigrated to Australia as babies – Dad from post-war Germany and Mum from India, where her father was stationed while serving in the British Army. It staggered me that, apart from my sister going to Japan on exchange in high school, 80 per cent of my family hadn't been overseas as adults.

I'd always been captivated by overseas travel, ever since Narelle Watt came back to primary school after three weeks away (not during the holidays . . . *I know!*) with a Mickey Mouse T-shirt from Disneyland. Not from a relative who'd returned from a trip, but an actual purchase made at an actual Disneyland in an actual United State of America. Even as a twelve-year-old I was jealous and from that moment on I couldn't wait to experience it for myself. (Travelling, not Disneyland. If I wanted to line up for hours surrounded by overweight Americans then I'd go to – well, I'd go to Disneyland.)

To me it's a choice *not* to go overseas, because nowadays, with such cheap flights and accommodation packages available, it's so easy. I understand why we didn't do it as kids; Mum and Dad both worked full time, and travel in the eighties wasn't as affordable as it is now. Also, there could be no greater living nightmare than dragging three children around the world. Kids are annoying enough in the supermarket; if I had to take three of them overseas I would have an aneurysm before I made it down the aerobridge. The mum in *Home Alone* wasn't forgetful, she knew that one less kid on the holiday was the smart move.

Nor have I ever understood the waste of money that is taking a toddler on an international trip. 'Let's pay to bring along someone who will be a challenge every waking moment and won't remember a thing.' I'll admit on occasion that's been me after a few too many resort cocktails, but that's my own money being wasted.

When I was twenty-five, which was as soon as I could afford it, I backpacked through Europe, expanding my horizons by seeing what Irish pubs looked like in Rome, Berlin and even Prague. The trip also taught me how to survive on a steady diet of jam sandwiches, ham and cheese sandwiches, or, to get some variety, jam and cheese sandwiches. It takes paying $33 for a tiny bowl of spaghetti outside a German castle to realise you always need a back-up plan. A plain bread roll soaked with a mouthful of Coke provides more than enough flavour and sustenance.

Since that first trip, I've travelled as often as I can, making me the man for the job of taking Dad to Europe. This in itself was out of the ordinary, because I'd never been the man for the job before. Ever. Unless that job was to get drunk at a wedding and tell the bride I had feelings for her, but for some reason there's not been a ton of requests for that after the first time.

———

Holidays are exciting. Counting down the days until take-off, constantly checking the weather at your destination, organising travel insurance because your parents have made you paranoid about getting everything you own stolen. I actually love the frustration of the final twenty-four hours, longing for the hellish long-haul flight to begin.

I had almost always travelled solo, because I relished the freedom. I loved knowing I could change plans on a whim, hearing about something cool and deciding to do it, or being able to ditch an annoying Brazilian backpacker who was going to get me killed by starting trouble in a bikie bar in Cusco, Peru. I had only travelled in a group for weddings, and resort stays don't really count. The toughest choice on a beachside holiday is what cocktail to have before midday (I always choose a mango colada, as mango is a breakfast fruit).

Travelling alone, I found the planning really easy, too. Typically before you book a trip you have a discussion about where you'd like to go and how long you might spend in each place. So it was a simple case of conferring with myself, having a few arguments, storming out, cooling off and then coming back to completely cave to my own demands. It's a system I've refined over many trips and it works.

But because it was Dad's first international trip, I mapped out the journey as slowly as possible so he could contribute to the planning and feel like he was as much a part of the trip as I was. I asked questions about where he wanted to go, what he wanted to see, if he'd prefer to drive or fly between cities. Then I'd leave it with him, giving him time to think about it, the idea being that the next time we spoke he'd have answers. Kind of like what usually happens with questions. But not with Dad involved. I'd ask, go away, only to return and discover he'd put no thought into anything. We basically hit pause the moment I left his sight.

After a few weeks of this non-decision I made a decision: that giving him time was pointless. I took to asking him directly then waiting him out until he responded, like a teacher waiting for a class to settle down, pretending they have nowhere better to be. I sat for hours at the kitchen table with Mum, sticking around their place much longer than I normally would, until he finally gave me answers.

The first question for any potential trip is where to go. The start was easy for us: Munich. Dad had family there, so at the very least we'd visit them. So that was a tick. Whenever he'd mused about Europe in the past, Big Ben and Buckingham Palace would almost inevitably get a mention, so London was also on the agenda. I put that as our last port of call so we could fly out of Heathrow. Tick. We were on a roll. All we had to do was fill in the blanks in the middle.

Everyone has different reasons to travel: to see another culture, learn history, meet family, continue to sully Australia's overseas reputation by climbing sacred monuments while completely hammered. From what I could gather, Dad wanted to see the main tourist attractions and that was about it.

There was, as I quickly discovered, far too much wiggle room. Everything between our arrival in Munich and departure from London was open for discussion. Except it wasn't a discussion, because Dad could not be drawn into giving his opinion on anything.

I sat at the kitchen table with my notepad, determined we'd get this trip mapped out before I left. I'd stopped in for lunch but was prepared to stay for dinner if that's what it took. Nothing shows resolve like eating two free meals.

'Alright, Tommy,' I said. 'Let's do this. Rome?'

'Yep.'

I put Rome on the list.

'How about Paris?'

'Yep, I'll do that,' he replied instantly.

Paris too. This was easy.

Then it got strange. 'I'd like to see Amsterdam,' he said.

I put it on the list, but was immediately concerned. Aside from drinking, Dad's as straight as they come. He once dropped my brother off at a party and advised him to 'stay away from the funny cigarettes'. So if it wasn't the hash then I could only assume he wanted to go for the red-light district, because I knew for certain we wouldn't be going to the Van Gogh Museum.

He had some momentum now. 'Stonehenge.'

'That's in England. We're already going there.'

'Colosseum.'

'That's in Rome, mate. You know that.'

'Oh yeah.'

'Prague?'

'Yep. Where's that?'

It soon became obvious that he was happy to visit every place I suggested. Athens, Glasgow, Dublin. Every single one was going into the ever-growing mix, because Dad had no appreciation of the size of Europe. He was saying 'yes' like all those cities were within an 800-metre radius. As though travelling to the continent was the same as going to Chadstone shopping centre for the day. 'Okay, we'll start at the Colosseum, then we'll go to the food court, and then head on up to the Blarney Stone next to David Jones.'

Hitting every city Dad said yes to was doable, but as I'd discovered on previous trips, it was a slog. Early starts and repeated airports, followed by rushing around all day trying to maximise every second to make sure you'd seen everything that you'd be asked about when you got home. It had been exhausting enough when I was in my twenties; I knew that pace wasn't for a sedentary man comfortable with his senior lifestyle.

Plus, city hopping is expensive. Our budget was hardly 'tuxedo-wearing Monaco bachelors'. Mainly because Dad's married. And the closest he gets to black-tie is a nice polo shirt.

In the end I made a captain's call: to never again use the phrase 'captain's call'. From all the options put forward, I decided we would go to Paris. My rationale was that I'd already been to Rome and if I was going to go all the way to Europe then

I should at the very least give myself something to look forward to. Plus, Paris had the added bonus of the Eiffel Tower, a landmark Dad was aware of, which is how it had ended up on our list in the first place.

So after much one-sided 'discussion', our itinerary read Munich, Bamberg (where Dad's family was from), Berlin, Paris, Caen (a town in France I'd tell Dad about later) and London.

As if deciding on the cities wasn't agonising enough, our next task was to work out how long to stay in each one. That can be a lottery at the best of times. There's nothing worse than booking a town for several days and hating it. You can't leave because flights have been locked in, or you're stuck in an awful hotel but can't afford to book a better one. Trying to stick it out rarely turns your feelings; you spend most of the time looking for validation as to why it's such a shit place. 'Yep, someone tooted their horn unnecessarily. This town is the worst. Never in doubt.'

But by now I knew if I involved Dad in this laborious process then he'd drag his feet so much we'd land in Munich with no plan at all. So for simplicity, and to avoid having a stroke, I booked everything myself and let Dad know afterwards. As expected, he was fine with it all.

The less involved Dad became with the planning, the more it was apparent that he was not prepared for certain parts of travelling. Like the travelling. He managed a few things, such as getting a passport, packing, and withdrawing a dangerous amount of foreign cash. Though all that was done with Mum's assistance, and even then I'd had to follow it up every step of the way. Which meant once we left and she was no longer around, I'd be picking up that slack and doing the work of two. I was not looking forward to being travel pregnant.

It made sense that the planning had been left to me, but I was slightly concerned. My last international trip had ended in shame and embarrassment. While I was used to those feelings, they generally didn't rear their heads on a professional level.

I had been booked to perform comedy on a cruise. I'd always wondered who took cruises. Planes exist; there's no need to step back in time. I bet passengers don't get taken down to the docks on horseback. I prefer travelling at 900km/h over a mode of transport that still talks about its speed in knots, a measurement that's deliberately vague so you don't realise how slow it is.

Perhaps what convinced me was the prospect of getting out of the Melbourne winter for some warmth, since this particular cruise was bound for New Caledonia.

The ship was leaving from Sydney, so the trip began with a short flight from Melbourne. As I sat on the plane with my seat reclined – it's okay, no one was behind me – I ran a mental checklist of everything in my luggage. Perhaps I should have done that the night before, because in a hurry it dawned on me, just west of Canberra, that I'd forgotten my passport.

I'd only thought about my flight, which was domestic, and not the actual cruise, which was international. I couldn't even fabricate a story that it wasn't my fault – that I'd been asked to present my passport as ID and not had it handed back, or that my butler had failed to put it in my carry-on luggage.

I couldn't believe I'd been so stupid. Even though it was a pointless exercise, I decided to at least show my face on the boat so I could officially be knocked back. Maybe being brave enough to admit that I was an idiot would buy me some brownie points with the company that had booked me. It didn't.

As I stood at the ship's customs counter the agent handed me a phone receiver. I took it, assuming it might be to talk to a superior about being issued a temporary passport or some other fictional document I tried to convince myself existed.

'Mate, what the fuck's going on?' These were not the words of a government official.

Blindsided for a split second, I quickly realised this was James, the man who had hired me. Thinking quickly, a skill that would have been handy the previous night as I packed, I thought of about five or six excuses as to why I didn't have my passport. 'Left it on the plane.' 'Fell out of my luggage.' 'Pickpocketed.' 'Accidentally grabbed my ASIO one for spying missions.' 'I'm gay, this is now a hate crime.'

But I figured I'd be honest.

'I forgot it.'

He hung up, and the customs officer told me what I already knew: I couldn't board the ship without a passport. She left out the part about me being an idiot.

My itinerary for that day was taxi, flight, taxi, boat for ten minutes, taxi, flight I had to pay for, taxi, home. It was the single biggest waste of a day in my life, and I've been to Docklands in Melbourne.

What made it worse was that I had always prided myself on being a competent traveller, that it was one of the few areas of my life where I could and should be trusted. Around friends and family I'd kept up the appearance of taking care of myself, but people weren't seeing me eat cereal for dinner.

I'd hit the jackpot with my friend Marie, who was a travel agent. That's the holy grail of the travel world. Sure, you can do everything yourself online, but travel agents know things, forbidden mysteries us mortals are not privy to, like if a flight you wanted to book really was full or if the airline was just holding seats for premium flyers.

Travel agents can call airlines directly. They have the secret phone number that gets you an actual living human. If I tried calling, it would be a four-hour exercise in futility, being put on hold so long that the music drove me to accepting the middle seat on a thirteen-hour flight. Travel agents make stuff happen. Stuff like Marie securing emergency-exit row seats for Dad and me just weeks before we took off, ensuring we didn't have to go through that lottery when we arrived at the airport.

I tried to sell Dad on how great the emergency-exit row was. On the 23-hour flight to Munich we'd have extra leg room, the ability to leave our seats without annoying anyone, and we'd be in charge of everyone's survival should the plane ditch into the ocean. All the benefits!

Dad's focus wasn't on the extra space, though.

'Twenty-three hours? Is there nothing faster?' he asked, as though if we slipped the pilot a fifty-dollar note he might take us the back way and get it done in seventeen.

I told him, 'No, I'm pretty sure the airlines tend to take the direct route.'

To finalise the booking, Marie needed to know who was sitting in which seat. It was arbitrary, since we could swap once we were actually on the plane, but I wanted to be nice. So, on my next visit home, at a family lunch for Easter, I asked Dad if he preferred to sit by the aisle or the window. Although I'd had to take the itinerary out of his hands, I thought I'd at least allow him to make this choice. But as he flip-flopped between the two options – aisle or seat – I realised I'd made a mistake: I'd given him options.

It would torment me for the entire trip, but this was the moment it first dawned on me that I'd saddled myself with the worst kind of companion: the wishy-washy traveller. They're 'I don't mind' personified, agreeing with absolutely every possibility that's put in front of them without really committing to any of them, until you feel like grabbing them by the throat and forcing them into a choice. Even if it was jumping the Turkish border into Syria to join ISIS, you'd be ecstatic they'd made a decision.

'Do you want aisle?' I asked Dad.

'Yep.'

'You're sure you don't want the window?' I followed up, because what sane person doesn't want the window?

'Okay, I'll take that.'

'Right. So you want the window?'

'Yep. I can talk to the birds.'

I took a deep breath, hoping that he'd see that as a sign of me needing him to be serious for a second.

He didn't see the sign.

'No – aisle. I can roll Jaffas down them.'

In the end I chose the window and gave Dad the aisle. Weeks earlier my brother Jason had said he was jealous of Dad and me doing this trip together, but after witnessing this deranged exchange at Easter, he admitted he wouldn't be able to cope with Dad for three weeks.

I tried to convince myself I was blowing Dad's non-committal attitude out of proportion; things would be okay once we'd actually made it to Europe. But my gut instinct laughed that off.

I knew that I was in for three of the most maddeningly frustrating weeks of my life, and nothing was going to shake that feeling. Outwardly I projected a sense of calm, but internally I was already sweating the trip. I had to talk myself into taking things one day at a time, and we hadn't even made it to Melbourne airport yet.

The trip was a big deal for my whole family. I knew just how far out of his element Dad would be, even if he hadn't realised yet. We grew up definitively middle class and unadventurous – three-week overseas holidays weren't a thing. Dad had a comfort zone that had been years in the making, and he was about to be removed from it in one fell swoop. If I told Mum on the phone that I wouldn't be able to make it to dinner at their place until 7 pm at the earliest, I could hear Dad complain in the background that he'd be eating after his usual time. Doing things 'on a whim' was not in our family vocabulary.

When we were kids, we only ever had the one TV and, when the plunge was taken to get a video recorder, there was no debate over VHS or Betamax – we were so late to the party, Beta was already off the market.

Dad went all out, buying a VCR with a remote control, an exceptionally new technology and one that showed we were buying at the top end of the market. Either Dad had worked a lot of overtime or the VCR had been on special, because splurges like this were unheard of. But the excitement was short-lived. Opening the box, we discovered that the remote control had a cord running back to the VCR.

This was a massive let-down, but it wasn't a surprise to Dad. He'd knowingly purchased a remote control with a cord, meaning you were 'remote' only as far as the cable length allowed, which, in our living room, did not include the couch. The remote would be placed on the rug in the middle of the room and you'd have to get up from your seat, walk over to this so-called remote control and pause/rewind/fast-forward whatever we were watching.

But the remote was new and exciting, so to avoid fights between us kids, Mum and Dad would designate the 'remoter' for the evening. That's right, we *wanted* to do it. Nothing could make it clearer how little novelty we had in our lives. It was an honour to be handed that work detail.

The remoter was confined to the rug, because it was quickly decided the trip from the couch was creating too much of a lag in remoting. I learned to look out for station promos at the end of the block of ads I was fast-forwarding, letting me know the program we'd recorded was about to return. Paying attention was a big deal, because if you missed hitting play in time Dad would groan and the whole family had to wait as you rewound the tape (no way we were missing six to eight seconds of a show). This was something my sister Michelle did far too often, and her carelessness cost her the job. I became Remote King. It was a perceptive appointment from Mum and Dad. Who knows how many of Hawkeye's antics on *M*A*S*H* we would have missed if it weren't for me.

The beverages in our fridge reflected our suburban tastes. Juice contained at the most 25 per cent real fruit juice. The flavour was almost always orange, though occasionally orange and mango would slip through. Sometimes apple and raspberry would appear if someone had gone nuts, or they'd accidentally grabbed the wrong one. Either way, it was a welcome change from the boredom of pretend orange. It wasn't until years later that I bought a real orange juice and realised pulp was a thing.

The preferred drink in our house was cordial – because it lasted longer. It was always orange and lemon, never Koola (green) or Red (red). Never. 'Too sugary' was the explanation, as if the citrus flavours had less sugar. I could tell who had made the cordial from the moment it hit my tastebuds; the sweet sensation of shitloads of sugar rushing through my body let me know it was a batch made by Jason or Michelle. Mum and Dad's cordial concoctions were always much, much weaker. Theirs was so watered down it left only a hint of cordial, like the scent of a perfume that remained in a room from someone who'd been in there hours earlier.

Still, it was better than footy cordial, which by my calculations is made at a ratio of 1 part cordial to 250 000 parts water. If you can taste flavour in footy cordial then you have a future in wine tasting or sniffing out truffles. I never understood why it was made so weak. Was there a football club that folded after someone blew all the funds on a decent strength cordial?

Once a year, for Mother's Day, our family ate out at a restaurant. Together with my grandparents, aunts, uncles and cousins, we'd head to Alasya, a Turkish restaurant on Sydney Road in Brunswick. This was exotic compared to our usual menu, but Dad was a huge fan of the banquet of meats, dips, meats, bread and meats.

One of the more exciting moments in our lives was where my sister and I shared a meal with Dad at the pub. At the time Dad was working as a laboratory assistant at CSL, a company that amongst other things made antibiotics and antivenin. He had picked up my sister and me from school, which he never did as we lived a five-minute walk away, and instead of going home, he decided to return to work drinks with us in tow. This was strange; I couldn't understand why we hadn't gone home, but it was an outing we'd never had before, so we weren't about to question it. Being a good father, he didn't leave us in the car but brought us inside one of the rougher pubs in Brunswick.

I loved it. I felt like a mini David Attenborough as I got to see Dad in his natural environment. He joked about his mates and made them laugh, but then was also the target of wisecracks and put-downs himself, which he enjoyed just as much. His behaviour was like that of my own friends, except this was Dad, who was usually telling us off for putting our feet on the couch.

He made his friends stop their game of pool so we could play (which at that age was just pushing balls around aimlessly with the cue) and bought us food. With my limited knowledge of pub fare I'd ordered toast, and when a steak sandwich arrived he even pulled the meat out before I had a chance to whinge about it, handing me the buttery toast while he ate what would have been a very cheap cut of meat. I didn't want the day to end, but after his eighth pot of beer Dad decided to do the responsible thing and drive us home.

Thursday night was fish and chips night. Traditionally it's on Friday, but Dad couldn't tolerate the crowds, so for our family it moved to a quieter night. I loved the trip down to the shops, being lifted up to the counter so I could place the order myself, reading from the note Mum had written. I don't know why it had to be written out, considering the order never changed: five pieces of flake, $2 worth of chips (a lot back then), dim sims and potato cakes. Perhaps the note informed the orderer whether the dim sims were to be fried or steamed, and whether soy sauce should be added immediately or at a later stage. Vinegar was never put on the chips, though, as I'd been reliably – and constantly – informed it brought on my asthma. My brother and sister would always ask for vinegar, but Dad would incline his head towards me, reminding them that ol' weak lungs couldn't handle it.

I shared a bedroom with one of my siblings for my entire childhood. First I shared with my sister, Michelle, then when we moved I was forced to share a room with my brother, Jason. He made it quite clear he was not into giving up his solo lifestyle by taping a demarcation line on the carpet.

I didn't experience the joy of having a room to myself until he moved out, when I was in my late teens. My brother decided it was time to leave after I came home blind drunk, interrupting him and his girlfriend watching TV. I stumbled in and passed out, almost making it to my bed. He started looking for a share-house the next day.

Mum and Dad never forced the issue of us moving out of home, happy to look after us as long as we contributed with both chores and rent (which I tried to pay with humour, a commodity not accepted as payment in the Rozenbachs household).

We had a garage, but much to Mum's anger it was always occupied by various non-running cars Dad and Jason were fixing. I'm not entirely sure what Mum's plans were had the space been available – an old upright piano she'd bought sat in the corner, but even if the space was clear I can't imagine her learning to play it out in the cold. She remained constantly frustrated, usually because when a car left and the space was briefly opened up it was replaced with another bomb or, even worse, once Jason covered everything in plastic and used the garage as a spray booth to repaint his car.

Dad and Jason were mechanical and I was not. I listened to their endless car talk (I still have an intimate, fairly useless knowledge of Ford engines), but when it came to physical participation the first time my cold knuckle smashed into a steel chassis rail I was back inside with Mum reading my Choose Your Own Adventure books for the fiftieth time.

Our house wasn't renovated until I was eighteen, the extension adding an extra room that we really could've used when my siblings and I were younger. By this time Jason was a qualified carpenter, so he built the extension. By comparison I was a metal-music-loving bookworm, and Dad thought I was a little on the soft side. So when he and Jason began building the extension, I decided I needed to step up and offered to help. It didn't go well.

My fear of heights meant it took me almost an hour to even work up the courage to climb up to the roof, where I had the idea that I was going to help put the corrugated sheets on. The moment I stepped off the ladder I was overwhelmed, hugging the roof with all my strength in case I should somehow roll off. I managed to crawl to the centre, as far away from the edges as possible, where I completely froze. I couldn't even make myself move to get back down the ladder.

Work carried on around me for about twenty minutes, until the roofing sheets reached my section and I either had to move or become part of the structure. So with my brother's assistance I managed to inch my way across the roof, my shaking almost dislodging the ladder as I reached my foot over the edge to the first rung, Dad holding it steady and talking me through the climb down like a policeman talking a jumper off a ledge.

Events like that didn't help my standing of not being particularly useful. My brother was physically enlarging the family home – I was a blubbering statue on the roof. It wasn't hard to work out who was the more useful son.

Until now.

Dad said goodbye to Mum like he was just off to the cricket. Mum wished us both good luck – for Dad to be safe and for me to be able to handle him for three weeks.

In the taxi out to the airport I felt overwhelmed by the idea of that amount of time with him. In the last twenty years the longest we'd spent together was going to the footy, and that was only around three hours.

I calmed myself by breaking the trip down. Three weeks wasn't that much. It was just 21 days. 504 hours. A mere 30 240 minutes. 1 814 400 seconds with Dad. That was all.

When we got to the check-in counter, I got my first real look at Dad's suitcase, which, it turned out, came from a bin. This sounds a lot worse than it was. He ran a mini-skip business, so bins had become his life. He'd bought the business in his later years and absolutely loved it. He often regaled me with stories about the Wollert tip, the landfill he dumped his skip bins at, recounting the time some guy did something or other there. As should be obvious by my vague recounting, I didn't really pay attention to these stories. I prayed he wasn't about to use the impending flight to tell me about the recycling section they'd recently installed.

He and Mum had built a thriving business partnership, Dad collecting the skips, Mum running an op shop. It was the perfect combination, Dad pulling items from the bin he figured had value, Mum selling them back to a vintage-loving public.

Years of experience taught him to look out for the most valuable bin of all: the divorce clean-out. Super friendly and chatty, Dad would always get inside info, including finding out when a couple had reached this terrible (for them) time in their lives. For Dad, it was the perfect opportunity to swoop. In a divorce many almost brand-new items get tossed. It was like Christmas. In a bin.

Which is how Dad got his suitcase.

It was enormous. Imagine your standard overseas-travel suitcase, then increase its size by a third, as though it had been on a steady diet of Krispy Kreme donuts washed down with deep-fried thickshakes. And it was the deepest red you've ever seen – if you happened to be flying above it, you could easily mistake it for the heart of a volcano. I didn't have proof, but I'd safely guess the suitcase had been the cause of the divorce in the first place.

Oversized, glowing red, yet Dad still thought to put a ribbon on the handle in case there was another identical one on the baggage carousel at the other end.

As we stood waiting, I asked him, 'Why did you choose such a big one?'

'Everyone said the one I tried before was too small.'

'What do you mean "tried before"? You've never been overseas.'

'Your mother and I did a dry run of packing.'

Apparently he and Mum had packed his suitcase a few weeks earlier, to see what he would need. Not two days out, as most people might do, getting a bit of a head start by packing things they wouldn't be using the next few days anyway.

I assumed then that they'd done a dry run with this monstrously large suitcase as well, but when I grabbed a handle to help Dad out, I realised that couldn't have possibly happened. It felt like lifting a small pallet of bricks.

'Jesus, Tommy, what's in this?'

'I don't know. Jeans, shoes, some jumpers.'

'Some . . . how many is some?

'Eight or nine.'

'What do you need that many jumpers for?'

'Your mother told me to.'

That explained why this warehouse on wheels was so heavy. I'd told him two jumpers would be sufficient, explaining that it wasn't a big deal wearing the same jumper two days in a row as we wouldn't be seeing the same people again. When I looked back at photos from my backpacking days, you'd think I'd only packed one T-shirt.

So a woman who had never travelled was giving advice to a novice about what to pack in his inner-city flat of a suitcase. Great. He probably had a dustbuster tucked away, 'just in case'. I made a note to ask Mum how she'd managed to get him to take her advice, when he never showed interest in anything I had to say, even if I had a ton of experience.

Not that Mum was immune; Dad would often ignore her solid advice. She'd tell him to put sunscreen on before mowing the lawn, only for him to return to the house with his nose redder than an alcoholic forced to drink his way out of a cellar. This went on for years, well after the Slip-Slop-Slap campaign was retired, so ingrained in Australians that it was deemed unnecessary. But not for Tommy. 'Bit of sunburn never hurt anyone,' he'd say.

The suitcase taken care of, we cleared customs without too much trouble, Dad proudly handing over his passport for the very first time. He smiled, then caught himself and unsmiled, ensuring he replicated the photo in the passport.

Once through security, we set about waiting to board, a necessary period of boredom. Usually I kill time by having a beer or two. Experience had taught me to cap any alcohol at two drinks, because of the trips to the bathroom it induced. Any more than two could result in me settling into my seat only to feel a trickle in my bladder. Not enough to require a trip to the toilet, but more than enough to keep me awake.

I'd also decided we'd keep the drinks to a minimum as Dad, trying to relay a sense of calmness by casually chatting about other flights on the departure board, had revealed his nerves with a couple of trips to the bathroom in the short time we'd been there.

I needed something to distract him. Thank you, duty-free.

As Dad and I made our way through the store, he marvelled at the range of products, the different sizes and, of course, their prices. Dad *loved* duty-free. He wasn't even a fan of shopping, begrudgingly taking Mum to the Westfield Shopping Centre in Airport West every Friday night, where he preferred to stand out the front of every shop with an ever-larger volume of Mum's bags. But here Dad was excited, marvelling at things he would normally never buy.

His favourite was the 4.5-litre bottle of Johnnie Walker, complete with a stand to assist in pouring a drink from such a ridiculously large bottle. It retailed for a mere $150. Or as Dad put it, 'Bloody cheap that!'

Not that he'd know. He doesn't drink scotch. I doubted he knew how much a regular bottle might be. It wasn't as though I visited Mum and Dad's and there were empty 4.5-litre bottles of Johnnie Walker strewn about the lounge room.

He was the same with the cartons of cigarettes, nodding knowingly as though he was aware how much tax was put on them. Even though we had Europe in front of us, Dad was loving the airport a little too much – the child playing with the box an expensive toy came in.

I got the sense he would have been happy to go straight back home after this thrilling new experience, not least because he was edgy about what was coming next. Aside from this being his first ever international flight, most of Dad's knowledge of foreign countries came via documentaries. And I enjoy a good doco, but as good as they are at teaching you stuff, they're also fantastic at planting seeds of fear in the back of your mind. Animal documentaries are the worst of all, particularly ones with names like *When Animals Attack, Animals in the Wild* and *Carjacked by Rattlesnakes.*

Weeks before a holiday in Thailand I watched a doco about the dangers lurking in tropical waters. I knew it was a bad move, but was unable to switch off. When I finally arrived in Thailand I was convinced every swim was going to end with me stepping on the spines of a stonefish and being injected with deadly toxins.

After a few hours of sitting on the beach, not daring to go in the water, I found the courage. Other people were splashing around without dying and that, coupled with the fact I'd had a few beers and the toilets were further away than the water, encouraged me to take the plunge.

My first foray in was nice. The waves were gentle and the water was warm (naturally so; I hadn't peed yet). I relaxed in an instant. That was why I had gone there. To unwind, not to constantly stress about dying in a really painful way.

Then an unidentified object wrapped itself around my leg. I immediately flashed back to the doco, convinced the odd, enclosed feeling around my leg was a jellyfish. I was sure I only had one or two minutes of pure agony left on this earth. During this panic I let out a squeal no man ever wants to, so loud and high-pitched it brought people running to the beach, looking for a six-year-old girl in distress.

Convinced these were my last moments, I looked down and saw the jellyfish's white body puff up, the '7-Eleven' on its side clearly visible. Realising my mistake, I was relieved. Shopping bags are rarely lethal. But I was embarrassed I'd screamed in deathly fear in front of everyone on the beach for, as far as they could tell, no reason at all.

These days I'm purely land or pool-bar based. Bit of alcohol never hurt anyone.

This would be Dad's first ever long-haul flight, quite the achievement for someone in their sixties. His longest flight had been from Melbourne to Cairns, but even that didn't really count, as it was broken up by going through Brisbane. I could run a marathon if it was broken up into 2-kilometre legs.

When Dad came to Australia from Germany it was by boat, which, although longer than most flights by about sixty days, was made easier by the fact that he was two years old and completely oblivious.

He had no memory of that trip, so it made sense he'd be intimidated by a flight of this magnitude, and I chose not to overload him with tips. I've always found that once people know you're about to fly they're quick to offer advice: drink lots of water, get up and stretch regularly, take your shoes and socks off and push them through the gaps of the seats in front of you.

I kept my suggestions to the most essential: the neck pillow. For me the neck pillow has been a game changer in the flying game. I couldn't talk them up enough to Dad. People use booze and pills to help them sleep on planes, and I respect that, but there's nothing like having something to support your head so you don't have eight hours of that repeated nod off–head bounce–startled wake-up. Or, if you go to sleep with your head to the side, stretching one side of your neck and leaving you in pain for the first few days of your trip. Neck pillows are the penicillin of the flying world, I told Dad. If someone doesn't use one, that person is a fool, plain and simple.

Dad chose not to use one.

This was typical; Dad was always happy to dole out advice, but rarely took it. Once, when I had a sore back, he suggested I sleep on the floor. Apparently a hard surface was just what me and my inflamed back needed. I knew it was dodgy information, but against my better judgement I tried it. As if the excruciating pain the next morning wasn't enough proof he was wrong, hunched over in pain I went to my osteopath, who confirmed, 'Sleeping on the floor's probably the worst thing you could have done.'

And so the man who'd never been on a plane longer than three hours said, 'I'll be fine,' ignoring the recommendation of someone who had flown to South America, one of the toughest flights anyone can have the misfortune to take. It's hard enough to get comfortable for two hours on a plane, let alone thirteen, and the neck pillow at least gives you options. I always try to get a window seat so the neck pillow can work as an actual pillow as well. It's a beacon of luxury compared to the hessian hacky sack excuse of a pillow the airlines hand out.

My only advice to those who choose to use one is don't wear them in the departure lounge. Unless you're a newborn, you can support your own head while awake. I understand the argument that people wear one because they're going to sleep on the plane, but sleep is hours away. You're going to have something to eat or watch a movie first. I don't walk around my house two hours before bed with my mattress strapped to my back in preparation.

Though I do wear a condom all the time. Never know your luck.

Proving once and for all how much of a novice flyer he was, Dad actually paid attention to the safety demonstration. It's a rite of passage to reach the point where you think you're too good/ experienced to listen to that. In my head it goes, 'Blah blah brace position blah blah oxygen will drop blah blah exits are located somewhere!' It probably wasn't the smartest approach, consider-ing we were in the emergency-exit row.

Just being on a plane at all had me concerned for Dad. I couldn't imagine him being able to sit still for thirteen hours. He's an 'up and about' kind of personality. A tropical holiday beside a pool would be his idea of a living nightmare, unless one of the resort activities was helping grounds staff with the lawn edging.

Dad's preference was to be permanently occupied. When I was growing up any downtime was considered laziness. You know, like sleeping in beyond 8 am on a weekend. Dad would do the vacuuming early on a Sunday morning just to annoy us kids, repeatedly banging the head of the cleaner against the bedroom door. I learned quickly that it was a shouting match not worth entering into, because he would know he'd won, and the adrenaline that coursed through my body would make going back to sleep impossible. So I'd learned to ride it out, knowing Dad would eventually move on, but not before making the carpet outside my bedroom clean enough to perform surgery on.

But he wouldn't have any choice on a flight to Europe, which is essentially a twenty-four hour prison stint. We'd be told when to wake and when to sleep, we'd be given the occasional stodgy reheated meal in a tray, sleep alongside a complete stranger, and once every nine to ten hours we'd be allowed to stretch our legs in the confines of a giant, impersonal concrete complex where our every step is monitored. There is always the possibility that you could get bumped up to premium economy for good behaviour, but I think that's just a legend people like to recount to give people hope. I've never witnessed it in real life.

The only way to pass the agonising minutes as we slowly made our way over the Indian Ocean was with the in-flight entertainment system. I had extra confidence the entertainment system was going to be a hit after Dad's excitement levels rose pretty high when he was handed a hot towel, and then peaked when this was followed up with a set of free headphones.

'How good's this!' Dad said, looking around in disbelief, elated because he'd received something for free (disregarding the fact we'd paid quite a lot for the flight) and because, I would safely say, they were his first ever set of headphones. At this rate the range of TV shows and movies available was going to have us celebrating with a bottle of champagne. Or perhaps a can of beer, once he saw how much a bottle cost.

Excitement aside, I was concerned about Dad dealing with technology. He has never liked it and will only accept it when he's left with no choice, like when the analog mobile phone system shut down. He reluctantly handed in his phone that was so old I'd forgotten how to send a text on it. Dad's certainly wouldn't be asking Siri for weather updates any time soon. 'Which one of those women is Siri?'

That's not to say Mum and Dad's house was a complete throwback to another time; they had wi-fi, but as I'd discovered every time I visited with a new or updated phone, no one could remember the password.

Dad was comfortable with what he knew, and anything else that could help make life more comfortable was waved off as something he didn't need. For example, he refused to believe in Teflon. Now, you might be reading this thinking, 'I thought Teflon was the non-stick material that coated fry pans and the like.' You'd be completely right. Dad claimed it was rubbish, and proceeded to scrub every Teflon pot and pan with steel wool, taking it back to bare metal, going from non-stick to incredibly high-stick. He was adamant Teflon didn't work, and saw that as reason enough for him to ruin all tainted products. Teflon. It may not wipe clean like it does in an infomercial, but it was a lot better than the scorched-black, exposed steel cooking trays in our house.

For this trip Dad had to get his first ever credit card. And not just his first ever *credit* card, but his first ever bank card, full stop. His reasoning was why would you ever want to go into debt to anyone? So carrying around a card created solely for debt made him uncomfortable. I had no doubt that the moment we landed back in Australia he would not only pay off his debts, but shred the card too. Then burn the shredded bits. Even trying to explain to him that EFTPOS cards were only using his own money fell on deaf ears; cards were evil and not to be trusted.

Instead of cards, Dad still used cheques. I've never owned a chequebook, as I've always found money a particularly good source of money. On the rare occasion I've needed one I simply go down to the bank and get charged a mere $8 for the privilege of them typing one up.

I didn't think cheques had a place in modern society, but as I discovered after doing a comedy gig at a lawn bowls club, not everyone agreed with me. Bowls clubs are not known as bastions of the modern world, but no one complains about it because their beer prices are also from 1982.

After the gig I was approached by the club treasurer to complete the transaction of money for services rendered. Generally payment comes in an envelope, or, if I'm lucky, someone might want to do the handover of cash via handshake. That always made me feel pretty cool, as I imagined myself in a gangster film. (Although it told me I wasn't getting paid particularly well, as you can't palm a wad of cash.)

On that occasion, however, I was confused, as the treasurer pulled something white from his pocket – the colour white doesn't appear in the cash realm. At a gig like this you might see something yellow, perhaps red or, occasionally, even the completely cool but highly impractical green of the $100 note. But white? The treasurer handed it over saying, 'Thanks, really enjoyed that. Appreciate you coming along, here's your money.'

I'd been handed a cheque. I looked at it, thinking, 'What kind of economy is this? I performed for you now, so I think it's within my rights to expect my payment to be as immediate.' If I had known it was going to be cheque, I would have done all the set-ups to my jokes and then delivered the punchlines in three to five business days.

I wanted to shout, 'You think my drug dealer takes cheques, you stupid old fool!?' Instead I smiled, thanked him and sent a text message to my drug dealer. He doesn't.

Dad's distaste for technology didn't fill me with confidence for the flight to Munich. But the in-flight entertainment system is one of the greatest inventions of our time, up there with the MRI and hypercolour T-shirts (who wouldn't want to know where the warm patches are located on our bodies?). And it isn't until it's gone that you really appreciate it; one time I flew from Athens to Bangkok with a broken in-flight entertainment system. All we had for thirteen hours was a map of the plane crossing the Indian Ocean. It moved at a rate of around one millimetre every twenty-five minutes, which, while completely mind-numbing, was still better than any Mariah Carey film.

So once we were underway, it was time to turn the thrilling hot towel–headphone quinella into a trifecta and throw a film into the mix. I informed Dad that before I went to sleep I would set him up with a film I knew he'd like – *Expendables 2*, an action flick with one of his faves, Sylvester Stallone. I told him that when it eventually finished he should get the attention of the cabin crew and they'd happily set him up with another movie.

'Yep, no problem,' he eagerly agreed, which from years of experience I knew meant he would do precisely nothing with the information I had just given him. Aside from staying awake and helping him during the entire flight, there wasn't much more I could do. Armed with two sleeping pills swallowed with my last sip of beer, I checked out of the flight for a few hours.

I will admit this wasn't the most responsible course of action I could've taken, considering we were in the emergency-exit row and tasked with aiding the flight staff in case there was a problem, but I figured if something catastrophic happened at this altitude the hosties could use my limp body as a test for the emergency slide or to help douse any flames.

Even with the pills it wasn't a solid sleep, but I managed to avoid about seven hours of the flight. From there I only had a few more hours to sit through before we arrived in the UAE for our stopover.

As I slowly woke, blearily looking across at Dad, I wondered what he'd been doing since his film finished, which I calculated to be about five hours earlier. I could see there was something on his screen, but it didn't appear he was watching. Maybe he was listening to music on the entertainment system, but I figured that was a deep technological dive beyond his capabilities. Perhaps on his first ever flight out of Australia he was able to admit he was out of his depth and had sought help?

As I shook off the sleeping-pill fog and came fully awake, I got a proper look at his screen. He was indeed in a section other than movies. As far as I could gather Dad had attempted to set himself up with another one but failed. Instead he'd somehow ended up listening to the Koran. In Arabic.

I've not lived at home for quite some time, but I believe Mum would have mentioned a conversion to Islam. Not least because Dad would have had to give up bacon.

Eventually we landed in Abu Dhabi for our stopover. For the first time in his above-age-three life, Dad was out of Australia and on foreign soil. Unfortunately for him there wasn't much to see, as we were in travel purgatory. Our stopover was only slated for two hours, which for a long-haul flight is a quick turnaround. I've had connecting flights delayed and then cancelled, forcing me to spend nights in places that would never be on anyone's bucket list.

The stopover was still long enough for Dad to expose himself as a first-time traveller. It's an unwritten rule that when you get off the plane in transit you are to act miserable, avoid eye contact and definitely not smile at anyone. Dad was like a budgie that had been taught to say 'hello', smiling and asking everyone he came into contact with how they were. Including the stunned cleaning and security staff waiting on the aerobridge. Judging from their reactions they'd never been acknowledged before, let alone greeted warmly.

His friendliness brought a smile to my face; seeing that Dad could be so innocent, maintaining a sense of politeness that most of us discard after our second-ever flight, I thought to myself I should follow his lead. But not right away; first I needed to shove my way to the front of the line to get into the transfer lounge so we could get decent seats.

As we sat waiting for our plane for Munich to start boarding, talk naturally turned to how the previous flight had been. Dad informed me he hadn't really slept much, which I found strange, as his ability to fall asleep anywhere he likes inspires great hatred in me. He could doze off on top of the speaker stack at a Metallica concert, only for the band to pause to ask him to stop snoring so loudly.

I assumed he must have drifted off for at least part of the flight, because it was a midnight departure and we'd been in the air for thirteen hours – that's a tiring stretch for anyone – but apparently I was wrong. With only one movie under his belt, I inquired as to what he had done to occupy the rest of his time (when he wasn't listening to the Koran).

'I counted how many people went to the toilet.'

I paused, taking it in.

'What do you mean, you counted people going to the toilet?'

'I kept a count of how many people went to the toilet.'

I was hoping his follow-up response would have a deeper meaning than that, but it was exactly what I thought. Rather than calling over a hostie and asking them to essentially do their job and set him up with a quasi-comedy you'd never watch on the ground if your life depended on it, he sat and stared into the semi-darkness, counting people's trips to the toilets.

Being unable to sleep for that long showed me just how nervous he was, but it also had me concerned for those passengers, not knowing some random man was watching them go to the bathroom. I made a mental note to ask him not to do that if we were sitting in a park in the near future.

But I understood Dad's anxiety. Even though I'd travelled extensively, I still felt the flutter in my stomach every time I got to the airport. For me it was more excitement than nerves, the thought of arriving in an unexplored city and imagining what it would be like. I still had worries, but they were about minor things, like whether I'd like the city, how I'd get from the airport to the hotel, and if it would be too early for a beer on arrival.

Dad didn't have any experience to call on. Being only two when he left Germany in 1949 meant his memories were foggy at best. I sympathised, remembering how I felt going overseas for the first time some fifteen years earlier, unsure of how a completely different country operated. Would I fit in? Could I cope with the language? Would I disgrace myself with my lack of knowledge of local customs? Fortunately, aside from not being smiled at for about three weeks, I eventually got the hang of England.

Dad and I sat in a comfortable post-flight silence, tired, looking at nothing, hoping the next leg started sooner rather than later. I don't know exactly what Dad was thinking about, but clearly he was fascinated by this exotic locale, because the first thing he asked me was, 'How many desalination plants do they have here?'

It was a strange question. Yes, the UAE was a desert climate, and they'd undoubtedly have them, but I'm not sure how he expected me to have the answer. Particularly as he knew my subscription to *Desalination Monthly* had expired years ago.

'Dunno, Dad,' I responded, and left it at that. I didn't want the conversation to keep going, as I wasn't sure I'd have the answer about the production of camel milk either.

Dad fell silent, and I pondered where a question like that had come from. Had he been waiting to ask it the whole flight? Was he trying to fill the silence? Or did it just pop into his head and he really wanted to know? This didn't really happen at home, but I guessed it was because Dad had such a ritual that nothing was ever out of the ordinary.

I sensed it was going to be a long three weeks.

When I was younger I loved spending time with Dad. My favourite outing together was our biannual trip to the tip. The moment Dad mentioned we 'might head to the tip next Sunday' I started to get excited. He probably didn't enjoy going as much as I did, because for him it meant gathering enough crap to put in the trailer to make it worthwhile. It might be pruning all the shrubbery around the house, or perhaps Mum was sick of the garage having more and more things packed into it and had demanded a clean out. But I couldn't wait.

I'd help Dad bring things to the trailer, but wasn't allowed to pack it. At that young age I didn't have the *Tetris* skills required to make the most of the limited space the trailer offered. So I stood back and watched, tossing on a branch or two that slipped off.

Once the trailer was brimming with crap piled so high it blocked all visibility from the car, it was time to stand back as Dad tied down the load. Years later, at my first ever adult job, packing boxes in a warehouse, I was taught by truckies during pick-ups how to tie proper knots for securing cargo. Dad used none of these. He would loop the rope around and over the trailer and rubbish about a thousand times, tying knots so tight they added an extra fifteen minutes when we got to the tip because no one could undo them. And we weren't allowed to cut the ropes because, as he'd tell me, 'Ropes don't grow on trees.'

But once the knots were undone, it was party time. I could throw rubbish as far as eight-year-old-humanly possible. Even though I wasn't allowed to help with the packing of the trailer, I made sure to pay close attention to where certain items were being placed. In particular, the breakables. The moment these treasures were exposed, I swooped in. Nowhere else in the world was I afforded the freedom to break things with, as I saw it, 'diplomatic immunity'. Glassware was the most fun to throw. Or seeing someone else's glassware on the tip pile, aiming whatever I could at it, and smashing it into a million pieces. All without getting in trouble! For a child it was like international waters, and I was a pirate on the high seas of garbage.

The tip wasn't all fun and games though. Well, not for the adults. When it came to reversing the trailer up to the pile of rubbish, there was immense pressure to complete it in one go. The Tip Guys who worked amongst the sweet, rotting stench all day would point to a gap leading to the pile and you'd back your car and trailer into that spot. Theirs was a smooth process, knowing exactly where to direct people so the tractor could come along and push your rubbish from one pile into a bigger pile. As a kid, it was majestic. I envied the Tip Guys. Until a time I saw one sitting on an old esky eating his sandwich surrounded by hundreds of seagulls, like a pungent remake of Hitchcock's *The Birds*. As much as I loved the tip, even I had to draw the line there.

Reversing a trailer is one of those skills you don't appreciate until you try to do it. Unless you own a boat or a horse, some people may never attempt it, making it something of a lost art. But if you have tried it, you'll understand how difficult it is. The idea of having to turn the steering wheel in the opposite direction of where you want the trailer to go is confusing enough.

In practice it's even worse, as the front end of the car goes in one direction, the trailer flies off in another, and you have to spin the wheel like you're in control of a tall ship.

Once, as I was enjoying the sophisticated, guilt-free pleasure of throwing breakables onto other breakables, I watched someone try to back a trailer into the space next to us. Except the trailer reversing towards me was coming at an acute angle. I stood back and watched as the car drove a good distance forward to reset the whole procedure, only to reverse so poorly the trailer nearly took out our car beside it. This was followed by one more poor attempt, which Dad halted by whistling for the driver to stop, lest there be a jackknifing and the trailer end up at a right angle to their car.

As a kid I had no appreciation of the art of the trailer reverse. Dad just backed the car in anywhere. Tips, driveways, down the street, wherever. He could do it, so I assumed everyone else could, too.

Turns out this guy couldn't. Even at that young age I could sense the pressure he was under. One misfire, that was okay. On his second go people started to notice. By the third attempt everyone had put down their rubbish to watch the spectacle of the man who couldn't reverse a trailer. This is what nightmares are made of.

But with a quick, 'Jump out, mate,' Dad took control of the situation. The guy sheepishly got out of his car, Dad jumped in and handled the wheel with casual aplomb as he backed the man's car in for him, perfect on the first attempt.

I was impressed, and proud that Dad had these skills this other man didn't. It was the early eighties; if he couldn't reverse a trailer I have no doubt his manliness was brought into question. Probably after he unloaded all the rubbish from his trailer he threw his testicles away as well.

As the years went on, Dad would let me tie down a section of the trailer, always double-checking my work so things didn't fly off on the drive down to the tip. Eventually we reached the point where I was allowed to hitch the trailer to the car. I'd completed this successfully a few times, until one day, in my haste, I forgot to push down the handle that activates the locking mechanism and secures the trailer to the tow ball.

I'd remembered to attach the chains to the tow bar (a back-up safety measure), so when the trailer slipped off it was still attached to the car. This meant the chains went taut as we pulled away, but slackened as Dad slowed. 'What's that noise?' quickly became 'JESUS, ADAM!' as a fully laden trailer slammed into the back of the car.

The car was fine, but Dad's trust in me was not. Trust further eroded when only weeks later, probably distracted thinking about the trailer, I got the pause/record button wrong on a TV show we were taping on the VCR, so that I recorded the ads and edited out the program. By the time I had regained Dad's trust, the tip had been converted into a recycling station and there was no more need for the trailer.

The tip remained a fond memory, but that love of spending

time with Dad was about to be seriously tested. Dad's compe-
tency in some areas, like reversing a trailer or removing Teflon,
made him think everything else would come to him just as easily.
Combined with his never really trusting my judgement, it meant
he never listened to my advice on anything, no matter how out of
his depth he was.

MUNICH

Twenty-three hours after we set off from Australia, we landed in Munich. I steeled myself for three weeks of solid, uninterrupted Dad.

He was excited to arrive, but not because we had touched down in Germany – he wanted to spend his money. Not in a high roller, 'let's buy $200 bottles of champagne and make it rain' kind of way, but more in a 'he and Mum made the effort of going to the bank and withdrawing euros and now he wants to spend this foreign money' way. They hadn't just exchanged a nominal amount to help him get by until he found an ATM, either. No, they'd decided to load him up with €2000 in cash, adding 'target for robbery' to his travelling repertoire.

I became suspicious when I suggested we should grab a couple of bottles of water and he didn't respond with 'why would I pay for something I can just get out of the tap?' He had the same logic with takeaway coffee – why would he buy

51

that when there was an industrial-sized tin of Nescafé Blend 43 sitting at home.

Like a modern-day Burke & Wills, we set off in search of water. On our way, Dad inquired, 'So if I give them fifty euro, they'll give me change?'

This question I put down to the lengthy flight and lack of sleep, for none of us are at our sharpest when we get off a flight. But even allowing for that, few forget the basic logic of the monetary exchange system we've employed over the last couple of centuries. I kept walking, thinking, 'You're not Amish! You know how money works!' but then again he still used cheques, so perhaps he didn't.

I answered, 'Yeah, Dad, of course they'll change it.' And to the amazement of no one but Dad, they did. Not that he took anything away from that experience; I think as far as he was concerned it had been a lucky guess on my part.

At Munich airport Dad confirmed his lack of technological prowess, as though there was any doubt, when he struggled with the tap in the bathroom. Considering we both arrived at the sinks together, he exited an inordinate amount after I did. When I asked what took so long he informed me he'd never seen automatic sensor taps. Apparently he'd spent the majority of his time trying to get a water flow – touching the tap, the basin, probably the mirror, completely flummoxed as all around him washed their hands with ease.

I did my best to take this on board, wondering how sheltered a life this man had really led. Perhaps he was indeed Amish. I made a note to keep an eye out for a butter churner the next time I was at Mum and Dad's.

Dad's cousin Markus and his partner Hans thoughtfully offered to pick us up from the airport. This would be an incredible gesture from a friend, let alone two strangers – albeit one of them a blood stranger – from the other side of the planet. I'd put airport pick-ups ahead of organ donation in terms of inconvenience, as I'd happily cough up a kidney if it meant not having to time a run to the arrivals area.

What would be the best way to respond to such an act of kindness? Walk straight past these people, pretending not to know them, and leave them waiting even longer than they already had. This was the 'prank' Dad had planned, probably concocted in the twenty-something hours he'd been awake. I instantly talked him out of it, explaining that Markus and Hans probably wouldn't find it as funny, having already committed to an airport pick-up. I also suggested his joke may not work, given they wouldn't notice it was us walking past as they only knew us from old photos from when I was a child and when Dad was much, much skinnier and had a beard rather than his now long-established moustache. Dad acknowledged the flaw in his plan and begrudgingly relented.

Dad has always had a great sense of humour, one of the traits I picked up from him that I'm actually happy with. He enjoyed pranks that were more playful than elaborate, like putting all the clocks in the house forward, causing Mum to think she'd accidentally napped for three hours. He probably could have let on a bit earlier, rather than watching her race around in a tizz to get dinner ready and then struggle to work out why none of us kids were hungry.

Or the time my uncle Michael was fixing his car and Dad, seeing a pile of parts underneath the engine, added some random bolts to the mix. This consigned my uncle to hours of frustration trying to work out where they belonged. The pranks were fairly harmless, though looking back at them it seems Dad just enjoyed wasting people's time.

His sense of fun wasn't always just for evil. When I was in grade two, my primary school had a fete, and parents were invited to create a stall to help raise funds. The standard ones were put forward – craft, lucky dip, baked goods. Dad one-upped all of these, getting an old car from my beloved tip (disappointed I wasn't invited) in the early hours of the Saturday morning and towing it to the school, placing it in the quadrangle usually reserved for downball/four-square or elastics.

His idea was simple: for $2 people could have the pleasure of smashing the absolute shit out of the car with a sledge-hammer. Fortunately nepotism was alive and well, and Dad gave me first crack at the car. Not that anyone seemed to mind;

an eight-year-old wasn't about to do much damage. I think it was fair enough anyway, since clearly he had stolen the idea after seeing my joy during our trips to the tip.

Not that there are records, but I'd go so far as to say that it was the most popular stall in fete history. Not just at that primary school; worldwide. People were lining up in droves, which certainly wasn't happening over at Scone Central. Normally reserved mums were standing atop the car, safety goggles on, dripping with sweat as they unleashed blow after blow onto this solid-steel sixties Toyota Corolla, their husbands watching on, nervously wondering where all this pent-up rage had come from.

When I was sixteen Dad took me to see Billy Connolly. I'm eternally grateful for that night, as it set me on the path I'm on today. He couldn't have known the spark it would set off inside me, but it changed my life seeing Connolly send thousands of people – including Dad – bananas for three hours.

I'm pretty confident Mum would've booked the tickets with her 'evil' credit card, but it was Dad who took me to the show. And perhaps he did see something in me, as it was just him and me, without my brother or sister. Or maybe it was just a coincidence. I'm just thankful he didn't take me to Bill Cosby.

Between that and his pranks, I'd picked up Dad's sense of fun, turning it into a career as a comedy writer and stand-up comedian. And like Dad, occasionally I took pranks a bit too far.

It's always cool to be the first and have everyone else follow your lead. I'm confident I am a trendsetter. Nut allergies are extremely prevalent these days – every child I meet is allergic to a nut of some kind. Every function is ruined by one or two children who can't even be near a nut, parties being shut down because someone who ate a peanut butter sandwich in the previous half hour tried to make their way onto the premises.

I am allergic to nuts, but anaphylaxis awareness wasn't a thing when I was growing up. Back in the eighties it was called whinge-ing. I've never knowingly eaten peanut butter; even as a toddler, I must've intuited that it would make me feel unwell. Not that my allergy meant peanut butter was banned in our house; my brother and sister ate it constantly, taunting me by shoving it in my face, the smell making me shudder. Unlike the children of today, I didn't carry an EpiPen, the lifesaving shot of adrenaline administered in times of anaphylactic shock. Nut allergies were so uncommon that they were not a thing, and I probably would have just been told to suck it up anyway.

When I eventually did an allergy test as an adult, to prove to my family I didn't make it up, Mum was genuinely surprised. She claimed it had never been an issue when I was a baby, when she would let me chow down on as much peanut butter as I liked. But I was a fat baby, so looking back now I don't think I was fat, I think I was just swollen.

I'd learned from Dad to never make a fuss. If there was any kind of incident, we were taught to deal with it without commotion and get on with our lives. And it was in this spirit that I refused to ruin my friend's fortieth birthday, even though I'd clearly eaten something that contained nuts. The telltale tingling sensation in my throat and mouth let me know instantly that all was not right, and this was confirmed when my eyes began to itch.

I briefly considered asking one of my friends to drive me to hospital, but word started spreading that speeches were imminent, so I decided I'd take care of myself. Pretending to walk to the bathroom, I did a phantom and exited the pub where the party was being held, hitting the street and considering my options.

Of which there was really only one: hospital. Actually, two. Death had fast become one of the possible outcomes, the allergy symptoms coming on faster than I had ever experienced before.

I briefly thought about hailing a taxi, but dismissed this idea, as I didn't want to burden someone else with my anaphylactic issues. Dad always taught me to take care of my own problems. I called an ambulance instead, considering situations like this are the very reason they exist.

By the time I spoke with triple zero, I'd managed to get myself to a side street, not even wanting to bother pedestrians on the main street the pub was on. As my throat tightened and I struggled for breath, I sat down on the footpath and slumped against somebody's brick front fence, the emergency operator urging me not to hang up or go to sleep, which I was desperate to do. I put that down to a lack of oxygen. Aside from not being able to breathe, I couldn't swallow, so was forced to spit on the ground, making me even less of a candidate for assistance from passers-by, because I looked like I was blind drunk.

After about five minutes I regretted not asking for any assistance. The way things were tracking I was going to be an inconvenience to *someone*, be it hospital or morgue staff.

It took nine minutes for the ambulance to arrive. That doesn't seem like a particularly long time, but to give it some perspective, if I'd synced up with the film clip of Guns N' Roses' 'November Rain', just as Slash stood in a field out the front of a church, ripping out his guitar solo, I was about to die.

When they got there, the paramedics went to work immediately, administering adrenaline and steroids, then loading me into the back of the ambulance. Adrenaline is what an EpiPen contains, which is why almost all allergy sufferers have one – me included. I didn't use mine as I'd made the super intelligent decision to keep this life-saving implement tucked safely away in my bathroom at home.

Once the paramedics had shut the doors and the ambulance headed off towards the Alfred Hospital, a sense of relief washed over me. I was probably going to live. But I still felt horrible, my swollen insides causing incredible discomfort, feeling like someone had rammed their fist down my oesophagus.

I closed my eyes as we sat waiting at a set of traffic lights, inwardly acknowledging that that incident was the closest I'd ever come to death. Another few minutes lying on the street and it would have been touch and go. That's when it dawned on me that we'd stopped at the traffic lights. I was in anaphylactic shock; was that not dying enough? How bad did things need to be for them to turn the lights and sirens on? It felt like my life wasn't as important to them as it was to me. The least they could do was run some red lights at double the speed limit, considering I was paying for the ride.

Emergency wards are impressive places to people-watch, particularly on a Saturday night when you're sober. By the time I was admitted my condition had stabilised, so I was able to pretend I was watching a *Twenty-Four Hours in ER* type reality show, live and unedited. I'd been given my own bed in a private section of the ward, which was a huge upside, as it was relatively quiet. The downside was I was hooked up to a computer that monitored my pulse, blood pressure, oxygen levels and heart rate, so I couldn't wander around and investigate the drunk dickheads carrying on.

Disappointed that none of my friends at the party had inquired about me, I started firing off text messages admonishing them. They responded that they'd thought I'd gone home, which was fair enough considering that was the exact thing I had led them to believe.

After a few hours in the ER I was well enough to go home, but the doctor recommended I stick around rather than risk the small chance of having a relapse at home. I thought about doing a phantom from the hospital, but instead took his advice. But even though a hospital is full of state-of-the-art technology, they don't supply phone chargers; my phone died after about two hours.

Boredom and I don't mix. With nothing else to focus on, I became fascinated by the computer screen giving me real-time updates of what was happening inside my body. As I studied the screen, I thought, 'I wonder what would happen if I held my breath?'

Looking around to confirm I wasn't about to be visited by a doctor or nurse, I took one deep breath and held it. Initially, nothing happened. Thirty seconds in, however, and things started to change. My blood pressure dropped. My oxygen levels plummeted. The peaks and troughs on the heart monitor became shallower and shallower. As I approached the one-minute mark, the decline continued gradually, yet I still felt totally fine.

Beeeeeeeeeeeeeeeeeeeeeeeeeeeeeeeeeeeeeeeeeeeep.

That was the constant, high-pitched noise that came out of the machine. If you've ever seen a film, you know it means someone has died. Out of the blue, the machine had flatlined me. There was no warning, nothing telling me, 'Back off, this had better not be a joke, mate, I swear, I'll flatline if you don't stop mucking around.' Just beeeeeeeeeeeeeeeeeeeeeeeeeeeeeeeeeeeeeeeeeeeeeep.

My mind raced, praying that once I started breathing again the machine would correct itself and stop the noise. Not only did the noise not stop, alarms started going off, alerting everyone in the ward to my predicament. As I sat amongst the screeching machine and wailing alarms, all I could think was, 'Oh, fuck.'

Hearing an alarm that usually means someone is in cardiac arrest, people came running from everywhere. When they reached me, they couldn't comprehend that I was sitting up, completely alert, watching it all unfold. I wasn't at death's door; more sitting on the comfy swing on death's porch with a nice glass of chardonnay. This group of medical professionals abruptly stopped, confused looks on their faces, as my state obviously contradicted the machine's foghorn.

One nurse took the lead. 'What happened???'

As an adult, there are times when you have to hold up your hand and take responsibility for getting something wrong. This was not one of those times. 'I don't know,' I told them, shrugging my shoulders.

Luck had it that Markus, a wisp of a man, was an English translator, which would prove very handy during our time in Munich. Physically he was the complete opposite of his tall, heavyset boyfriend Hans, a baker. Both were very friendly and warm, and we felt relaxed as we chatted about our flights, Hans making as much conversation as his limited English allowed.

We hopped into their VW Golf – Markus easily, Hans snugly in the passenger seat – and I wondered if everyone in Germany drove a VW out of loyalty to the Fatherland. Despite being a small car, surprisingly Dad's suitcase fit into the boot, even though it meant mine had to ride between the two of us in the back seat.

As they drove us from the airport into Munich we passed one of many service stations dotted along the highway, prompting Dad to ask our hosts, 'What's the price of LP gas?'

It would have been one thing if he'd asked about petrol, but LP gas? None of the vehicles he owned ran on gas. Perhaps he had kept an eye on the price back home, in case on our travel he came across some dirt-cheap LPG, thinking he'd make a killing chucking some in his massive suitcase and selling it in Melbourne.

Markus and Hans dropped me and the Wolf of Liquid Petroleum Gas Street off at our accommodation, a small Airbnb apartment in the heart of Munich. We agreed to meet up with the boys a little while later, once we'd settled in, unpacked our bags and freshened up.

Dad seemed disappointed with the size of the apartment, perhaps expecting a sprawling, warehouse-type loft. He seemed shocked someone could live in something so pokey, but everything was compared to the three-bedroom house on a quarter-acre block he was used to. I told him it wasn't a big deal since we'd be spending the bulk of our time sightseeing and the apartment was basically just for sleeping. Though I did note that if it was raining and we were stuck inside, we'd be in each other's pockets. While Dad went to the bathroom to wash his face and change shirts, I made sure to check the weather before we headed back out. We were going to be okay.

Our first foray into Munich was relaxing, being shown around by the boys. We strolled through the Marienplatz, the market square in the heart of the city. Dad seemed pretty impressed as we walked along, taking in the nice, clean city that is Munich. We had no plans of our own, so were happy to be led around by our hosts, acclimatising and walking off our jetlag while they pointed out various things of interest, like the town hall and Mary's Column. Nothing lets you know you've arrived in Europe like a religious figure on top of a big 400-year-old pillar in the middle of town. In my backpacking days I would've thought it was perfect for climbing after a night out.

Travel inevitably involves a visit to a place of worship, whether it's to honour a god or just out of curiosity. Europe is no exception, with cathedrals hundreds of years old drawing visitors by the truckload, including the Frauenkirche (Church of our Lady) in Munich. I was curious what Dad would make of the churches here, because he had always been vehemently anti-church, having turned from Catholic-school-attending altar boy to openly agitated whenever the Pope appeared on TV. 'Bloody bastards,' he'd say, to everyone and no one.

From an early age, Dad would tell us he thought they were money-grabbing grubs. Although he admitted he was heavily influenced by regularly finding himself on the receiving end of a whipping with a nun's belt. I was surprised to learn that nuns could be so violent, but more so that they wore belts. As a kid I imagined them to be like Batman's utility belt, complete with rosary beads and quickdraw holy water.

Mum tried to raise us kids as Catholics, but it fizzled out when we moved house and my sister and I had to enrol in the nearby state primary school. Only our older brother had to go through the communion/confirmation rites, back at the Catholic primary school near our old house. Peace be with you, sucker!

On my previous trips I'd always visited a couple of churches in the first few days, then became bored with them and stopped. This time around I had to make sure the churches we visited were of high quality, because if I bombarded Dad with any old run-of-the-mill cathedrals he was just as likely to cut loose with a tirade about how they're all a bunch of rich paedophiles.

I'm not a huge fan either – of churches or paedophiles – and there's no way I'd ever visit a church in Australia except for a wedding or christening. But overseas they have a sense of history to them that you just don't get in a country like Australia, because we came so late to the world party. In Europe churches have a magnificence that draws people into them, regardless of their denomination. I'm also more inclined to have a look knowing I can leave whenever I want, without having to sit through my friends' self-written vows. I guess the ornate detail is also a drawcard, the churches decked out to show riches and wealth – effectively the casinos of their time.

As we entered the Frauenkirche, Dad held his tongue. He didn't know his cousin or his boyfriend well enough to let fly with a rant about priests just yet. Plus, he looked genuinely impressed by the most magnificent and grandiose cathedral he'd ever been in. Over 600 years old, the cathedral had somehow survived the Allies' bombings of World War II relatively unscathed.

Dad stared in awe at the intricate carvings covering the interior, work that would have taken gifted craftsmen thousands of painstaking hours to complete. As we stood in rapt silence, I thought maybe we could go to churches after all; the skills of the labourers and the sheer size and detail that graced these elegant structures would override Dad's distaste for religion.

After a couple of minutes of Dad taking it all in, and me taking in Dad taking it all in, he leaned over and whispered, 'I wonder who cleans all this?'

If you'd asked me what I thought Dad might say in that moment, that question would not have made my top 250. Why would it? There were so many other, better questions. When was the church built? Who did the carvings? Under what conditions would they have worked? He could have asked anything, but what Dad decided he really needed to know was who cleaned the place.

Rather than being impressed by this extraordinary feat of medieval architecture, he'd have been more excited to be introduced to the cleaner. 'Dad, this is Johan Klauss, the head cleaner. He can't speak English so if you want to find out how he goes about his business you'll have to mime vacuuming or dusting.'

As we continued around the church I suspected Dad was looking for power points or hoping to catch a glimpse of a Dyson neatly tucked away in the 500-year-old crypt.

On our first night in Munich, we ended up at the famed beer hall the Hofbräuhaus for dinner. Dad was in his element, excited by the litre-sized beers and vast offerings of schnitzel (a delicacy of the region, so I couldn't play the 'try something local' angle), and surrounded by English speakers.

We sat on a communal table with a couple from Pittsburgh. Dad befriended them immediately. Within half an hour of introducing himself he was trying to convince them to re-invent their lives.

Dad had changed jobs late in life and loved it, taking a redundancy from his job manufacturing antibiotics, which he'd had for over thirty years, and moving first to window cleaning and then on to the mini-skip business he still owned. Because it had worked out well for him, it stood to his reason that it would be the same for everyone else.

Even though he'd known them for barely an hour and had no idea of their circumstances, Dad implored them to start anew, because life was too short. That was Dad at his finest, confidently dishing out advice with abandon because things had worked out that way in his particular situation.

He even exchanged email addresses with his new American friends (Mum's address – he wasn't that far down the technology track), reminding me fondly of a time when I'd do that with almost everyone I met while backpacking. It didn't matter if I'd spent a whole week with someone or just two hours, I'd be convinced the friendship would continue on way into the future. Only to find myself years later pulling a scrap of paper from amongst maps and tickets forgotten at the bottom of a backpack and staring quizzically at 'jeff_badboy84@hotmail.com'.

Long after Markus and Hans had left, Dad and I partied on, letting the night get away from us, more than happy to enjoy some beers with some other Aussies in celebration of us making it back to Dad's homeland. We didn't get back to our Airbnb until late at night – way past Dad's bedtime – and a little worse for wear.

I have to admit the excitement of being overseas had gotten to us, and we both started the next morning hungover. Not a new experience for me on an overseas trip, but sharing it with Dad was. In terms of our relationship, we'd gone from a leisurely 3km/h to standing up in a speeding convertible Lamborghini. I hadn't slept in the same house as Dad for at least fifteen years, and just like that we'd become BFFs. Well, for three weeks. BFFFTW, as it were.

I'm a huge fan of living alone. I had loved my first sharehouse, but the perfectly balanced functioning-alcoholic ecosystem we'd established there was destroyed when my friend Steve moved out at short notice and a guy named Lee took his place. Within days I had decided Lee was the worst human being on the planet. He had an Eminem tattoo that wasn't the result of a failed bet, he went to work and left the front door open so anyone could come in and steal all my stuff and, worst of all, he rolled up one leg of his jeans to the calf. I couldn't run the risk of people seeing us in public and thinking we were friends. So, with my pant legs both at the same height, I resigned myself to finding a place of my own.

I thought I would hate living by myself, that I'd be lonely, but within months I was in love with it. My mess was my mess – if I wanted to clean it up I could, but if I didn't that was okay too. The smells would let me know when the time was right. I watched what I wanted on TV. I didn't have to put pants on for hours longer than usual. And I discovered that drinking alone sounds a lot worse than it actually is.

I lived by myself for nine years and loved it. I knew at some point that would change, that one day I would (hopefully) move out with a girlfriend, but I was very comfortable with my lifestyle for all those years. Suddenly gaining a mid-sixties housemate wasn't something I'd planned for, even if it was just for a few weeks. But I felt I could handle living with Dad, as we were only going to be in the accommodation in the mornings and at night, so surely it couldn't be that difficult.

For his part, Dad had never lived alone. He was still living in his family home when he married Mum, they moved in together straight away and added three kids into the mix in rapid time. Really rapid time. I still can't bear to think about the thirteen-month gap between my sister and me. Jesus, Dad, give Mum a break.

By the time Dad was twenty-eight he was living in a share-house with four other people, an adult and three kids, but because it was his house whatever he did was considered okay. By the time I got out of my bedroom in Munich he was already up and about – even though we were in a completely differ-ent time zone and our body clocks hadn't adjusted yet, he still managed to be an early riser. But what I wasn't expecting was that, having only just used the bathroom (or more precisely, the toilet), he'd decided he didn't need to shut the door after-wards. This led to a very one-sided discussion about why I didn't appreciate it and how he might want to think of others (me) in the future.

With that awkward conversation out of the way, I gave Dad first use of the shower, while I looked for things for us to do around town. Before I'd even worked out how to get into the city from our apartment, he'd somehow showered, dried and dressed for the day.

I grabbed my toiletries and headed into the bathroom, only to be met with a fine dust on every surface. Either Dad had developed a severe cocaine habit (without losing an ounce of weight) or still used talcum powder long after everyone else knew of the damage it does to your lungs. The talc was everywhere. His regimen appeared to be to fill the airspace entirely and walk through it as though he was being deloused in the fifties, allowing the talc to settle on – let's say the 'humid' – parts of his body.

Talc had always been one of Dad's idiosyncrasies. For all I know Dad's hair and moustache might not even be grey; it's probably just talc he hasn't washed out. The other thing he swears by is wearing a singlet, tucked into his undies, 'to keep your chest warm' no matter the temperature, a trait pushed onto me and immediately abandoned the moment I was old enough. Amazingly, since giving up the life-saving singlet, my pneumonia count still stands at zero.

His talc of choice used to be Old Spice. It made gift purchasing the easiest thing in the world; birthdays, Father's Days and Christmases were simply Old Spice talcum powder, year in, year out, without fail. These days it's no longer on the market, and Dad was forced to resort to Johnson & Johnson's Baby Powder, which, even though it's the thought that counts, is way too low rent to give as a gift. One Father's Day I managed to source some Old Spice talc on eBay. As he opened it I stood by proudly, like Marco Polo having returned with exotic spices from the Orient.

———

Munich sold Dad the dummy in almost every respect. It's a relatively small city, not unlike a miniature version of Melbourne, so there were hardly any crowds, and it was easy to navigate on foot because most things were close to each other. Plus our tour guides, Markus and Hans, took us on the most direct routes. When we weren't walking, we were being driven around.

I knew Dad was thinking, 'Europe is easy!' He thought I was a liar. Because previously, no matter how much I prepared before going overseas, the one element that always brought me undone was the amount of walking involved, and I'd warned him about that.

I'd like to think that I walk a fair amount in Melbourne, but it's usually a casual stroll to the supermarket or the pub. Living in the inner city means I don't travel long distances, either, as almost everything I need is close by. But experience had taught me that overseas, walking can easily lead to soreness and niggly injuries, because you go from almost nothing to circumnavigating the earth on foot.

I never helped myself with the walking, as I'm not one of those travellers who can wear running shoes with casual clothes. Being overseas is no reason to give up your dignity by wearing jeans with Mizuno runners suited to running a marathon. My preference was to remain cool, walking around in casual sneakers. Yes, I always paid a massive price for that, but what cost for coolness?

Some travellers are completely unfazed by fashion, apparently just walking into a Kathmandu store, surveying everything, and saying, 'Yes!'

Weeks prior to departing Australia I had recommended to Dad that he start walking, to get some miles into his legs and acclimatise his body to what it would be going through in Europe. He took my suggestion on board as he always does. He smiled, said 'yes', then completely ignored it.

I pushed my case, but each time he argued, 'I walk,' even though this was completely untrue. I wasn't talking about strolling around Westfield at Airport West with Mum, or hitting the aisles of Coles on a Thursday night (supermarket shopping replaced fish and chip night once we all moved out). He drove a truck for a living but made it sound like he was a postman delivering a farming region's mail on foot.

Everyone has a kilometre or two in them, but it's backing it up day after day that had me concerned for Dad. After two days in Buenos Aires I could barely stand, a combination of hours of walking and an extremely poor choice of footwear. I had shocking blisters, my knees hurt like I'd been attacked by a bikie for not repaying a debt, but I didn't have the luxury of sitting in the hotel for a day or two to recover. I'd waddle my way out of the accommodation and onto the street, aching with every step, slowly working myself into a rhythm until my body warmed up and the pain eased a little. And that was at a time when I considered myself really fit. Unless walking to the fridge for seconds of leftovers (so, fourths) burned calories, Dad was not fit.

He drove everywhere in Melbourne, an option that wouldn't be practical when we were in a major European city. Even public transport usually meant stairs. Unless we hired a mobility scooter, Dad was going to be walking.

Every few days I'd check in with him to see how the preparations were going for the whole trip, but I'd also ask where he was at with getting his fitness up. He kept saying he'd been doing the walking, but Mum would undo him and tell me the truth. I was frustrated, firstly because I knew it would become an issue on our trip, and secondly because he was flat out lying to me.

It was a 'thing' with Dad that he lied, but usually it was so blatant that everyone would laugh it off. I'm sure we've all been guilty of making light of something we're not interested in doing. The problem is it doesn't actually address whatever the problem is.

In our house there was a ritual of Mum telling him to get ready to head out of the house and Dad yelling out, 'Just putting my socks on!' That was his joke. It must've done Mum's head in hearing it day after day. If I was her I'd have taken those socks and used them to strangle him.

Even as we were first preparing for the trip, I knew finding things to do was going to become an issue. Not liking anything at all tends to eliminate possibilities at a fairly rapid rate, and a continent with such a rich history gave Dad an almost limitless supply of things to turn down. So far we'd had a superficial look at Munich, which was right up Dad's alley. A quick look at an apparently dusty church, or finding out about the history of another building without having to go in.

I'd known for a long time what Dad's interests were. Or more to the point, what they weren't. The turning point had been when I gave him a book about cricket. I'd chosen it for his birthday/Father's Day combo present, the two days generally falling within a week of each other, allowing me to get by with only one gift. It was book-shaped, as books generally are, meaning he knew long before he'd opened it what it was. The only surprise would be the subject matter.

When Dad opened it, I could immediately tell by the lack of excitement on his face that he wasn't a huge fan. I was as annoyed as an eight-year-old can be, chastising myself for getting it so wrong. I'd gone rogue and paid the price. Old Spice talc was foolproof! I knew that. I knew he didn't read. He can read, he just chooses not to read books. They were Mum's domain; she read every night, tearing through books at an incredible rate while the TV was on and still managing to engage in conversation with us about what was happening on the show. It was quite the feat. Dad reads the newspaper in the morning with his coffee and that's it. I can say whatever I like about him in here knowing he'll never read it and, so long as Mum doesn't say anything, I'll be safe.

I've never liked to throw people under the bus, but that cricket book was 100 per cent Mum's fault. At that age I couldn't have scoured the bookstores alone, and wouldn't have had the funds to pay for the book either. She'd known him for a lot longer than me, so it also would have been nice to receive some guidance. Maybe she had offered some advice and I'd insisted on buying the book, thinking I knew how to win Dad over.

If you asked Dad what he'd like for any upcoming celebration, he'd say, 'Don't get me anything.' Some people would take that as torturously misleading, but Dad genuinely meant it. Nowadays I know it's a slab of Crown Lager, no matter what the occasion, but as an eight-year-old that wasn't an option. Not that I couldn't buy it; it was the early eighties and almost anything went. I just wouldn't have been able to carry it.

Beyond reading the paper, from what I could tell Dad didn't have a lot of interests. In the early days I'd have said it was the footy, as we went to see Carlton almost weekly. But as I grew older I assumed it was for my benefit, as he no longer supported a team, cynical about the modern game and what it had become. He saw it as soft, over-structured and boring.

He didn't like one-day cricket because he claimed – without offering any evidence – that it was 'rigged', like some kind of low-level truther. Even as a kid I didn't think that sounded right, but he stuck to it so hard that I began to doubt myself. He once had a love for boxing, long since passed, the Muhammad Ali era a peak that no other fighters could reach.

Though I struggled to find what he liked, I definitely knew what he didn't like. The arts were not for him, having never shown an interest in theatre, architecture, gardens, live music, painting, dance, literature, sculpture, poetry or history. I've never known him to go to a museum, probably because when you think about it it's just a 3D book that you have to walk around, and I knew where he stood on both books and walking.

Knowing all that, the first day in Munich I'd been playing on easy mode. Having locals to guide us meant Dad had been more inclined to go wherever they took us, as he didn't want to be rude to people who'd given up their time. Plus, in the early days of a trip, everyone tends to be more open to looking at everything; two weeks into a trip I'd find myself thinking, 'If I have to look at one more ancient relic I'm going to smash it like I'm back at the tip.'

I knew Dad would have felt a similar honeymoon effect, but that it would fade fast. I would have to choose our adventures carefully, because he would be prepared to put himself through far less than I was in the name of learning (which wasn't a lot); the extent of Dad's curiosity had been reduced to the trivia underneath Carlton Draught bottlecaps.

The Hofbräuhaus had been an easy sell, so if all tourist attractions had beer and schnitzel then we'd be fine. I had my fingers crossed that when we got to Paris the Louvre had introduced a pot and parma night.

Armed with all this information about Dad, I chose wisely for our first solo excursion: the Dachau concentration camp.

It would be educational but it wasn't a museum as such, so I figured Dad would be okay with it.

We wandered through Dachau in relative silence, recognising the horror that was perpetrated there. I had visited when I backpacked around Europe years earlier, and it was an overcast day once again, which seemed right. It's not a place that deserves sunshine. On the main grounds it looked like any old prison that had been shut down – iron gates, barbed-wire fences, guard houses – but it's pretty obvious a place has a heavy history when even school groups are solemn.

A desolate atmosphere pervaded. The showers. The room containing the ovens. The piles of shoes belonging to completely innocent people. Each scene was more confronting than the last, ramming home what sick and depraved things went on there.

As we sat on the train back to the city, I asked Dad what he thought. He responded that it wasn't much of a surprise as he'd heard so much about concentration camps as a young boy. I asked when that had been, knowing Dad had left school when he was fourteen, and I had only learned about it in the later years of high school. He told me his mum used to talk about the camps at home. This went a long way to explaining why he's never fazed by anything, because why would you be when you've grown up with knowledge of the Holocaust since you were a small child?

———

Before the close of business, Dad wanted to get to the post office to send a birthday card back home to Mum. This would be the first time they wouldn't be together to celebrate the occasion. I was blown away by this, though I shouldn't have been – neither of them ever travelled for work, so where else would they be mid-October? As a comedian I'm used to regularly being away from home and have missed plenty of birthdays, Christmases and other, lesser celebrations that I'm not terribly upset about, much to Mum's annoyance.

Post office located, we walked in and, after browsing for at least thirty-five seconds, Dad chose what he thought was the perfect card, just the right blend of happy birthday wishing and mocking of age. He wrote his message inside and then excitedly addressed the envelope, getting to write 'Australia' on it for the first time ever. He was briefly stumped by what to write on the back for the sender's details, laughing, 'It's the same bloody address!'

Our senses of humour couldn't have been further apart. Even though I'd worked that out the moment he turned the envelope over, I decided to let him have his moment. 'It is too.'

As we walked out the front to post it, he was exceptionally proud, even though I pointed out the assistant spoke English so well we may as well have been back home. Dad ignored me, content to taste the sweet German gum on the stamp, placing it carefully on the envelope and putting it in the box we were told to, on its way to surprise Mum.

With him so satisfied by this achievement, I decided to keep quiet about my distrust of foreign postal services. A package I sent home from Rome during my backpacking days never arrived – photos, souvenirs, hash-tainted trinkets. Sent back for safekeeping and to lighten the load, the package never made it, which I'm still disappointed about. They weren't of value to anyone, so it's unlikely they were stolen, but they were my memories.

I didn't tell Dad because I wanted him to feel confident that his nice gesture for the woman he loved would work out. Also, I didn't need to be lectured on Italians and their work ethic.

The two of us needed to get a move on, because we were due to have dinner with some of Dad's extended family. This was one of the big reasons for the whole trip, so to make sure it went smoothly Markus and Hans were picking us up at our apartment to drive us out to the suburbs. Walking down the streets of Munich, as we neared our place, Dad casually asked, 'What night's bin night?'

Even after the last few days with him, this question took me by surprise. In all my time travelling I'd never considered bin night. It was someone else's problem; I was merely passing through. I'd never considered him a naive person, and while I knew jetlag left you foggy, I was fairly sure it didn't make you simple.

I could smile at his questions on the first day, about who cleaned the church and whether you got change when paying with euros, but this was another level. Clearly he'd been thinking about it. He must've seen a bin out. Or perhaps he'd seen several bins, in which case he could have assumed bin night was that night. Or, as anyone else in that situation might think: it doesn't matter. Nothing on our trip would change because of this information.

When we got back to the apartment I checked my *Lonely Planet* and there wasn't a single section on bin nights, an oversight I'm sure they didn't correct for the one person who has ever required that information.

We both got ourselves ready for dinner thinking about bin night. Dad wondering when it was, me trying to work out why he wanted to know. And how did he expect me to know? I had done quite a bit of research for the trip, but not to that level. What other information would he need? What time the street sweepers would come through? Which night the local council met? If Mrs Schwarz's cat was tagged?

I expected Dad to interrupt my shower any minute to ask me whether I knew if our pilot from Abu Dhabi to Munich had been left-handed.

In the last few days, Dad had asked questions and displayed behaviours that were peculiar, to say the least. I'd not noticed any of this back home, but maybe I wasn't around often enough. I didn't recall any meaningless questions in my childhood, but would any kid? Everything Mum and Dad said I considered normal, because I had nothing to compare it to.

When I was young, my home was my universe, and Mum and Dad were my all-seeing and all-knowing gods. Until the one day I visited a parallel universe and realised all wasn't what it seemed.

Jonathan's family seemed very much like mine, which is why we'd bonded. One day he invited me to stay for dinner, and it was a big deal. (In primary school, this is getting to first base. A home run is the coveted sleepover.) This is when I discovered the earth was round.

As we sat for dinner, I felt welcomed in the extra seat and space that had been created for me at the table. I waited patiently for everyone else to start eating, so as not to disgrace myself or my family. My brother had had friends stay for dinner at our place over the years; I knew the conversations that went on after the friend left. 'Did you see the way he helped himself to the butter?!?'

When Jonathan's father, Mr Toohey, wondered, 'Where's the sauce?' I saw this as an opening and leaped to my feet, ready to prove what a gracious guest I was. I headed to the pantry to grab the sauce and triumphantly bring it to the table.

'It's in the fridge, mate.' There was a small amount of knowing laughter, but I barely heard it over the sound of my mind exploding. Jellied legs held me up as I opened the fridge, unsure whether I was about to be the victim of an elaborate condiment-based prank. Sauce in the fridge sounded weird, but then Dad had pulled off some pretty odd 'pranks' in his time, so I couldn't be too sure. The fridge light revealed it wasn't a gag; the sauce was indeed right there in the fridge door.

So many questions ran through my mind. Why was it there? What else from the pantry could go in the fridge? Did this mean I could cool down hot chips as I ate them? I had seen the future.

Like Columbus returning to the Old World, I came home keen to show off my discovery. After our next meal I eagerly cleared the table, sneaking the sauce into the fridge. At our next dinner I sat, not really interested in my food, waiting for my chance. I'd set the table, deliberately forgetting the sauce. I could see Dad looking around the table before asking, 'Where's the bloody sauce?'

I leaped from my chair, cocky, throwing a look at my brother and sister to let them know I'd handle this.

'It's just right here in the fridge, Dad,' I said as I opened the door and got it out. I proudly returned the now chilled bottle of tomato sauce to the table.

Dad picked it up. 'What's it doing in the fridge? Doesn't belong in there; belongs in the pantry.'

And just like that I was back to being a flat earther.

When the trip was confirmed, one of the first things we organised was meeting Dad's extended family. He had aunties, uncles and cousins on his mum's side who he'd never met. I hardly knew my dad's mother, so meeting her immediate relatives wasn't on any bucket list I'd constructed over the years. As Markus and Hans drove us through what could have been any middle-class suburb in the world, I steeled myself for some serious boredom. The tree-lined streets, modest houses with yards and the occasional trampoline took me back to visiting friends and family in my childhood.

As a child I dreaded the visits to my grandparents' house. Every Saturday morning, after the weekly supermarket shop, we'd head over to Mum's parents for what was probably about one hour but felt more like three or four months. It was nothing personal; I liked them, but their house was how I imagined life to be like under a communist regime. It was completely devoid of any current pop culture, the technology was at least a decade behind, and it seemed no one cared that the TV didn't have a remote control or any red hues, rendering cartoons almost unwatchable.

Going outside wasn't an option either. The house was built on such a steep block that any attempt at sports resulted in the ball, and the participant chasing it, gathering excess momentum and slamming hard into the back fence. Funny as it was when it happened to my brother, we all decided it wasn't worth the risk.

Instead I created my own 'fun', such as locking the bathroom door with no one inside. I knew full well the door's locking system – a button pushed into the knob that would pop out and unlock when you turned the knob – shouldn't be activated on exit, because it could only be unlocked from the inside. But I wanted to see what would happen. Which was exactly what I'd thought: the next person who needed to use the bathroom couldn't get inside.

This brought up the question of who had used the bathroom last. All sibling fingers pointed to me, but I played dumb as to how this freak accident of engineering occurred. The adults were forced to give me the benefit of the doubt. 'It could happen to anyone' they reasoned, aware it had never happened to anyone.

Eventually Mum's cousin was hoisted through the tiny bathroom window and unlocked the door from the inside.

Visits home to my parents are still trying, Mum filling silences by updating me on people I've never met. The blank look on my face lets her know I don't care, but she ploughs on defiantly, informing me, 'Val from number seventy-three is having trouble with people parking on her nature strip again.' I'd remind her I don't know who Val is, as I haven't lived in the street in twenty-five years, but Mum always viewed facts like that as mere speed bumps on the irrelevant-information highway.

Meeting family went against everything Dad had stood for my entire life. 'I wouldn't know them from a bar of soap!' was the cry we'd hear whenever we'd talk about relatives from Germany. Dad always dismissed any thought of meeting them in Germany or letting them visit us if they happened to be in Australia. He reasoned they were strangers, so what was the point of caring about them?

But once he had committed to the trip he really didn't have too much choice. It would be a fair slap in the face to travel halfway around the world, be in the very same city, and not bother getting in touch. It also helped that my cousin had met the same relatives a few years earlier, and there was no way Dad was about to let anyone show him up.

On the drive through Munich's suburbs, Dad was clearly nervous, but as was his style he didn't want to let on. His outwardly calm demeanour was undone when I told him he had a speck of dried blood on his face from a shaving cut – he fired back, 'Leave me alone.' It wasn't quite lashing out, but it was enough of an overreaction to tell me meeting these 'bars of soap' meant something to him. Instead of telling him he should relax a little, I decided to let it go, adding to the legend that is The Greatest Son in the History of Earth.

Walking into a stranger's house on the other side of the world, we could not have had a warmer reception. We were shown into the dining room, adorned with family photos on the walls, trinkets gathered over the years spread about on various shelves, and even an owl figurine, which every mum seems to have for some unknown reason. Our hosts did everything they could to make us feel welcome as we sat down for afternoon coffee, tea and cake. Not that I'd have expected anything else; they were hardly going to go to the effort of having us over and then make us watch *Who Wants to Be a Bavarian Millionaire?* Still, a potentially cold situation was instantly comforting, like sitting on a warm toilet seat on a fresh morning.

I wasn't entirely clear who was who in relation to Dad. There was Hildegunde, whose house it was, and Inge, who knew Hildegunde enough to be let in the house. She may have been a neighbour, but since we were there I guessed she was a relation of some sort. Both used Dad's full name, Thomas (pronounced *Two-muss*), which I enjoyed for its endearing, childlike connotations. I couldn't remember the last time I'd heard him called Thomas. I mostly called him Tommy or, if it was a formal occasion, Tomato.

For the first time in his life, Dad had aunties, uncles, cousins. It was something I took for granted and never even thought about; I'd had all that extended family from the moment I was born. Barring the two years aged from zero to two, Dad hadn't.

A few relatives, Kirsten, Federico and Margo, had also made their way from Nuremberg, almost two hours away. That sounded like a bit of an effort, but I guess their thinking would have been that Dad and I had put in twenty-four hours of pain to make it there, so a drive down the highway wasn't a huge ask.

Instantly the talk turned to how much Thomas looked like

his parents, Dad quietly relishing his chance to be the centre of attention. Their English was amazing, except for Herbert, the family patriarch who looked as though he'd survived the war. The Franco-Prussian War of 1870, to be precise. He was an ancient man, prone to blurting out whatever he liked at volume. I wish I could have understood it; it had the cadence and strength of something particularly un-PC.

Amongst themselves they would slip back into German, to quickly discuss a question that had been asked or to explain something to those with a weaker grasp of English.

Then, from out of nowhere, Dad started conversing in German. My dad. Tommy! Two-muss! Tomato! He spoke German!

I knew my mum was bilingual, because she spoke Greek with her parents. Though she didn't grow up there, her parents kept speaking Greek when they arrived in Australia, and she'd learned it that way. Often my grandfather would say things to me in Greek, my blank face a solid indicator that I had no idea what he was on about.

But Dad? A German word or phrase like 'Achtung' or 'schnell, schnell' might be haphazardly tossed about during our childhood, but as we quickly learned they were mostly things he'd picked up from *Hogan's Heroes*. But presented with the opportunity to join in a conversation, it came back to him. It was probably fifty years or more since it had been required, so he wasn't fluent or expansive, but as long as the conversations weren't held at any great speed, he understood enough to translate.

I needed to know what else he was hiding. Creative dance? A love of poetry? The ability to watch a reality TV show without saying 'this is bullshit!'? He really was an enigma.

Once Dad's German-speaking abilities were established, the chats slipped into long exchanges I couldn't understand. I had to wait until there was a natural break before someone would translate it all for me. Turned out Frau Wilhelm from number seventy-three was having trouble with people parking on her nature strip again.

While we were there, Dad took the opportunity to call home and wish Mum a happy birthday, using all his inner strength to keep it from her that he'd sent a card. He was as excited as a proud child about to give his dad a cricket book for his birthday.

We had arrived at around 4 o'clock on a drizzly October afternoon and as the chat hummed along it wasn't long before the sky darkened, heading towards night. Yet as we sat in growing dimness in the dining area, the lights were still to be turned on. It wasn't dark, but if you were driving you'd strongly consider turning your headlights on. Reading would have been a struggle.

I wasn't alone in that thinking either, Dad's eyes connecting with mine in the near darkness, letting me know he thought this was pretty strange as well. I wasn't sure if this behaviour had been carried over from the blackouts during the war (habits can be hard to break), but before long it was dark enough that if I'd owned night-vision goggles I'd have put them on to safely pour a cup of tea without scalding myself.

There was a lamp next to me. Above the table hung a seventies brown-plastic light fixture. They were clearly aware of lighting. I doubted they usually went to bed when the sun disappeared, only staying up after dark when Australians were visiting.

Fortunately, by the time the photos came out, someone had stumbled their way through the pitch-black and found a light switch.

The live Ancestry.com session that followed really drew Dad in, discovering so much about his mum as a young woman. He was seeing new photos of her and asking questions he'd never been able to. It was a lifetime of stories in one night, Dad finding out about his mum skipping school to go on picnics in the park and driving her friends to dance halls even though she didn't have a licence. Things his mum probably didn't think were memorable or noteworthy enough to convey to Dad, but he might've heard about if he'd had blood relatives around to fill in the blanks.

When I was younger I loved hearing from aunts and uncles about naughty things my mum had done when she was a kid, and Dad revelled in hearing this stuff about his mum for the first time. I felt for him, realising that a part of him must've always hurt, never having the opportunity for extended family when it was happening all around him for his kids and his wife.

Not that he'd ever admit to it, but for the first time I saw in Dad someone who did care about family, and in particular his mother and where she came from. He'd spent as long as I could remember walking around with a tough exterior, impervious to feelings, but at that moment he couldn't hide it. And what I liked the most was that he didn't try.

Darkness came eventually, but this time it wasn't lighting based. I should have known it would be impossible to have a few generations of Germans talking about the past without there being a skeleton in the closet. Or quite a few skeletons, as it turned out. Without any sense of shame it was revealed that on my grandmother's side a number of family members had fought for the German army in the first and second world wars, including my great-grandfather. I don't want to turn this book into an encyclopaedia, but for context, it's important to know that from the early 1900s up until around 1945 the Germans were not known as the greatest bunch of people on the planet.

Genealogy websites always boast about the family history they can uncover, so people can bore everyone to death with stories of 'Uncle Finbar, who worked the docks in County Galway, made his way to Australia after thirty-two of his brothers died in a potato avalanche.' They never came back saying, 'Aah . . . yeah . . . your grandfather was . . . intheGermanarmyinWorldWarTwo! Sorry! You asked!'

Hearing about my great-grandfather shook me; I hadn't expected that, and it took some of the shine off the fun night we'd been having. It must have been even worse for Dad, since he was a generation closer to it than me. No one wants a recent dark past. If some relative happened to go on a rampage during the crusades, well, that's far enough back that it almost sounds like a footy-trip anecdote (with a few more sieges). What I'd heard was recent history and still affected the present day.

I knew I'd have to sit with the information a few days, until I could digest it and let the feelings of dismay pass. I couldn't change what had happened. I took comfort in the knowledge that at least Mum's side of the family wasn't like that; from all reports Great-Grandpa Pol Pot had been a really nice guy.

We said goodbye, Dad promising to keep in touch with his new-found family. He seemed happy to have finally been to a family function that was actually his family and not in-laws.

On our last day in Munich, Markus and Hans took us for a traditional Bavarian breakfast: a meal of sausages, soft pretzels and beer. Dad and I were bemused by the beer. It would never work back home, because Australians can't be trusted and everyone would be blind by lunchtime. Dad couldn't have been more excited though, taking to the idea like someone who loves beer being offered it at breakfast.

Dad seemed genuinely happy. He'd met family, found out more about his mum, had beer for brekky and generally enjoyed Munich, even though the bin night puzzle was never solved.

We finished up with Markus and Hans, saying goodbye and a heartfelt thanks to our fantastic and helpful hosts, safe in the knowledge that even though we'd spent so much time together over these last few days we'd probably never see them again.

Our next destination was Bamberg, three hours north of Munich, the town where Dad was born. Not that he remembered living there, but it felt right to at least spend a night or two there on our way through to Berlin. Having seen how he'd reacted to meeting his relatives, I was now curious to see Dad's response to checking out where he came from. Before, I would have predicted it to be a stonewall of indifference, but now I thought he might be pushed into an over the top emotional display. Like a shrug, or an affirmative nod.

As we set off to hire a car for our drive to Bamberg, I noticed Dad was walking considerably slower than previous days and started looking sore. More to the point, he started to sound sore. He did his best to push on without complaint, which didn't mean he was silent; instead of talking, I could hear involuntary grunts, moans and mutterings under his breath, which told me he was in trouble. I offered to stop, but he turned me down as that would be a sign of weakness, something he's dead against. Every time I suggested we take a breather he responded with, 'I'm fine, I'm fine! Nothing wrong here!' The 'here' being said with as much strain as if he was in the middle of throwing a 30-kilo shotput.

Despite his denials, walking with a gait like a baby giraffe was proof he wasn't fine at all. His tactic of pretending to window shop – something he would never do back home – became more frequent. His critical error was stopping before noticing what type of shop it was, meaning his reasons for the breaks were becoming wilder. I became pretty suspicious when he loitered outside a wig shop, asking, 'How do you reckon I'd look in one of those?'

The constant pausing didn't worry me, but I was frustrated by the outlandish excuses he was concocting. For a man with no interest in architecture he suddenly wanted to admire every building in Munich, big and small. If he admitted he was hurting then we could both do something about it. I was more than happy to stop the moment he called for a rest. But that wasn't Dad's style. He came from an era of 'deal with it and move on'. His own father, Roland, had walked out on the family when Dad was six years old and, as far as I could tell, while Dad never let it go – he was determined to be a better father to his own kids – he never dwelled on it. I didn't hear him talk about his father until I was in my teens, when he'd say he didn't allow his dad's departure to cause him any lingering concern because, 'What else could I do?'

It's that same attitude that meant Dad never went to the doctor. Once, he broke his wrist changing the tyre on his truck.

Most people, faced with a seized wheel nut that won't budge, might use a hammer to hit the tyre lever and exert some extra force to release the nut. Not Dad – he used his hand. Which, in turn, broke his wrist.

The break was only discovered after almost a week of constant pain, not at all helped by the fact it was his left hand and his truck is a manual, meaning every gear change was causing him incredible pain. He'd tried to strap his wrist to ease the pain, but somehow his remedy of a bandage with rubber bands around it didn't solve the problem. Rubber bands. Because even though he'd wrapped his wrist in a bandage from the chemist, his expert mind figured a bit of extra stability in the form of rubber bands would do the trick. I'm not sure where he got that idea from; perhaps he asked one of the doctors at Officeworks.

Eventually he did end up at the doctor, who diagnosed the break and ordered surgery. He now lives his life pain and rubber-band free.

It's just the way he saw life. It wasn't okay to complain. RUOK Day wouldn't sit well with him. In his day men didn't talk about their feelings or show any form of pain, physical or emotional. He'd be more of an advocate for UROK Day, where people around the country get together to be told to 'shut up and get on with it'.

He wasn't a fan of the sook. When I retired hurt in under-12s cricket after copping a ball to the thigh and walking off the ground in tears, unable to carry on, I knew he was disappointed.

What he didn't know was that it was part of my master plan to wait out the good bowlers and come back on to the ground when the chumps were bowling. Thus making me look like a hero who'd returned from death's clubroom door to post a decent, against-all-odds innings. But thinking back to that incident, I can understand Dad's perspective. I could have carried on, but chose the easy path.

He took things too far the other way. Just because you shouldn't sook doesn't mean you shouldn't say something if you are genuinely hurting. I had made a point of slowing down our walking pace through Munich after overhearing him on the phone with Mum at our relatives' house. He told her I walked really fast. I wished he'd said it to me instead of her, so that I could've adjusted my speed earlier, rather than having to eavesdrop to find out what was really going on. But even my slower speeds were still causing him problems.

I would admit I did walk fast, but that was entirely down to one person: him. Wherever we went as kids I basically had to maintain a quick jog to keep up, constantly hearing 'hurry up!' over my heavy breathing. Now the tables had turned and suddenly he wasn't such a fan.

Hurriedly walking as though a street-market meat stick was rapidly passing through my digestive system wasn't the only trait I'd picked up from Dad. He had a sense of urgency in everything he did, which, against all my better judgement, became a part of my life too.

He instilled in me the attribute of always being early, which in and of itself is not bad, but Dad took it to the extreme. When I was a teen he'd be content to sit in the car for hours before I needed to be picked up from whichever event he'd dropped me off at. He'd sit there like he was on a stake-out, doing the crossword and probably counting how many people went to the bathroom.

As a fifteen-year-old, sneaking out from the Hot Trax blue-light disco in Moonee Ponds for a cheeky Peter Jackson extra-mild cigarette should have been an exhilarating moment. Instead it was ruined by flashing high beams and a tooting horn from across the road. Dad whistled, summoning me across the street to ask why I was outside the venue so early. It was a question I could have put to him, considering it was an hour and a half before the scheduled closing time, but after half a hip flask of Southern Comfort I decided silence was the better part of slightly tipsy valour. I mumbled something about 'getting fresh air', then skulked past my friends' laughter straight back into the venue.

His earliness set me on a path of urgency for everything I did in adulthood, an unnecessary anxiety entirely created by him. Don't get me wrong, people who are constantly late are worse than incessant sniffers, but I'm so far the other way I panic if it looks like I'm only going to be nine minutes early. I have to constantly remind myself to take things in, slow down, be patient. All because the words 'HURRY UP! COME ON!' have been ringing in my ears since childhood.

Watching (and listening) to Dad struggle to walk down city streets was the first time I'd seen him as old. Not being around him all the time meant it crept up on me, like looking at an old photo of myself and suddenly realising how much closer my hairline used to be to my eyebrows.

I was in a quandary; on one hand, the way I'd been taught would have been for Dad to suck it up. If the situation had been reversed, when I was growing up Dad would have let me suffer for not listening to his advice, teaching me a lesson. Like when you're a kid and your parents tell you not to touch something hot, and you touch it anyway and holy mother of fucking god you may as well have reached into a volcano. But even if you had third-degree burns you get no sympathy. 'Told you not to touch it,' would generally be the follow-up.

I was caught in the middle. I didn't want to punish him for not walking before leaving for our trip like I'd recommended (even though it would have been nice to get a little payback), but if I openly asked him how he was going, he would lie anyway. I decided to split the difference and over the coming days I would walk just far enough that I could see he was starting to hurt, then pretend I was lost or doing up a shoelace. Which left Dad thinking either I was an idiot who couldn't read a map or tie his shoes properly, or knowing exactly what I was doing and going along with it anyway. I prayed it was the latter.

———

We picked up the hire car, a white C-Class Mercedes station wagon. It's a run-of-the-mill car in Germany, but better than anything Dad had ever owned. He was impressed by some of the luxuries, ostentatious extras he'd never had, like power windows and air conditioning. When I informed him the car also had satnav and heated seats, he almost blacked out. Thankfully the leather bucket seats would have made the experience an extremely comfortable one.

Dad never spent big on cars, as he considered them 'a waste of money'. My childhood memories are of our 1974 Holden HQ Kingswood with vinyl seats that stuck to your skin in summer like industrial velcro. Any sudden movement would result in the removal of all skin from the hamstring and rear-of-knee region. Its belt buckles became so hot that if you didn't pay attention your leg would be branded with a mirrored Holden logo.

Summer wasn't the only season that provided dangers. Come winter the car leaked every time it rained and, alongside the temperature of the five bodies inside, created a fogged-up interior that only a rag or sleeve on the windscreen could rectify. The water also added to an overall damp odour that regularly made me car sick.

As was the custom of the day, both Mum and Dad smoked, their addiction to nicotine clearly overriding any concern for their son's asthma. Our car was a constant cloud of cigarette smoke, which, combined with the dampness, made any winter drive like travelling inside a mobile bong. Second-hand smoke wasn't seen as a health issue back then, so Mum and Dad didn't think they were doing anything wrong; though it should've become obvious when I was the only child in grade three with a nicotine patch.

Between my asthma, my parents' smoking and Dad's talc use, it must've been a race to see what killed me first, a thought that used to keep me awake at night as I lay under my asbestos blanket. Thankfully Mum smoked Alpines, a menthol cigarette, which meant the coroner would at least be in for a minty-fresh surprise when he got to my lungs during the autopsy.

Through my entire childhood, we never had air condition-ing in a car. Ever. I understood not having it when I was younger, because in the seventies it was a luxury. By the mid-eighties, however, it had become standard across most models. Dad just never chose those. It wasn't required, not when you could 'wind your bloody window down'. If I followed this instruc-tion in summer it would result not only in a constant blast of furnace-temperature air to the face, but allowed the ash from the cigarettes Mum and Dad held out their open windows to blow right back into my face.

After the Kingswood we 'upgraded' to a roomier but older 1971 Ford Fairlane. It had air conditioning, a bonus of getting the high-end model, but unfortunately for four-fifths of the family, the refrigerant gas had long since run out, rendering it useless. Despite our pleas, there was not a hope in the world the gas was getting replaced.

We begged for a newer car but it always fell on deaf ears, Dad's argument being, 'It sits in the driveway most of the time.' I understood this to a certain extent, but countered that when it wasn't in the driveway, we sat in it. It would have been nice to arrive at a family event and not be the only ones soaked in sweat, having spent the whole trip praying to arrive so that we could get out of the car and finally cool down in the 40-degree sun.

Dad and I emerged from the rental place, ready for our drive to Bamberg. I drove a few minutes down the street, searching for somewhere to pull over so I could set up our satnav. Stopped at the roadside, I realised within a few alarming seconds I didn't know how to access it. My car didn't have satnav, and there was no chance Dad's did – he still used the physical *Melways* road atlas, cheerily choosing that moment to inform me, 'It's never let me down.' He'd buy a new *Melways* every year to allow for construction of new roads, housing estates and suburbs I'd never heard of. At least his completely outdated analog technology was up to date. I liked to imagine he camped outside the newsagency overnight, waiting for the latest edition to be released.

Getting assistance from the hire place wasn't an option, as I'd driven a few kilometres down the road before finding somewhere to pull over. Returning would have involved back-tracking for quite a few blocks and if a one-way street or some other obstacle appeared that forced us to turn off, then we'd be completely lost. My stubbornness was also a huge factor, as there was no way I wanted to admit to Dad that I couldn't work out this technology. I'd drive us into the Mediterranean before I conceded I was lost.

The satnav screen sat on the dashboard. I tried pushing on it with my finger, but could tell immediately it wasn't a touch screen. Dad did the same and I told him, 'I don't think it's touch screen.' I knew for sure it wasn't, but I figured if I began with 'I don't think . . .' it would soften my message.

I was looking around the car desperately, knowing we needed a map of one sort or another or it was going to be a nightmare of a trip simply getting out of Munich, let alone to another city three hours away. While I scanned the car, Dad attempted touching the screen again, as though perhaps he hadn't pressed it hard enough earlier. I reiterated strongly that it still wasn't a touch screen.

The stress building inside me, I searched for a button that said 'GPS system all located here'. This was when Dad gave it one last attempt, almost pushing his finger through the screen and into the engine bay. 'Dad! It's not touch screen! You're going to break it!'

I didn't understand what was wrong with him. Why was he going back repeatedly, as though pressing harder would solve our problems? 'Sorry Mr Rozenbachs, the screen in this model of Mercedes was designed to be pressed to the point of almost breaking before activating. Lucky you had your dad with you or you'd have been stuck in Munich.'

I was frustrated that I couldn't work out something as simple as a satnav, but mainly because I'd snapped at Dad even though he was only trying to help.

'Sorry Dad, I don't know what's going on. Why can't I fucking find it?' The tone in my voice conveyed my defeat. I tried to regain my composure, but the longer we sat there the more I felt like I'd let him down. I was suddenly back to being the kid who couldn't be put in charge of anything. The difference from the trailer chain incident was Dad's reaction: he was surprisingly calm.

'It doesn't matter,' he said.

It did matter to me; it was the most important thing in the world. I knew it shouldn't have been, but then I wasn't brought up under a regime of calmness and tranquillity. It's not like I lived on a knife edge, and I'm sure my parents knew when to soothe a worried child, but this 'she'll be right' attitude didn't exist when I was growing up. It was more 'do it properly!' or 'what did you do that for?'

When I was nine years old and put a nectarine from our tree through Mrs Smith's window next door, Dad didn't shrug his shoulders and say, 'Doesn't matter, these things happen.' As I recall, his reaction was quite the opposite. Perhaps I shouldn't have said a bird flew into the window, then hastily changed the story to a cricket ball being struck from the other neighbour's backyard (which would have been quite the shot, to clear our backyard and into Mrs Smith's). The changing story didn't help my case, nor did the number of nectarines sitting under the smashed window. The smack on the legs and a week without television let me know we weren't cool with such acts of wanton vandalism.

Sitting in the car, desperate for a way to make the satnav work, I wondered where Señor Chilled beside me came from. Perhaps Dad's demeanour was the result of no longer having to worry about me all the time, allowing him to be the person he was before he had kids. Before he got put in charge of someone who thought throwing nectarines at a window was going to have anything but a negative outcome.

It's why I think kids should be shown videos of their parents before they had children, when they were young and carefree. That way they would get to understand that it's their fault their parents are short-tempered and frustrated all the time.

Fortunately we were saved when, like a bolt from the blue, I remembered how to operate the satnav from something I'd seen on *Top Gear*. No, not casual racism – I recalled an episode where the satnav on this type of car was operated via a big dial on the console, next to the gearstick, which controlled all the car's functions, including the life-saving maps. Relieved and proud I'd finally worked it out, I dialled in our destination, stopped Dad from again attempting to crush the screen with his finger, and set off.

———

I didn't have to worry about Dad smoking on this drive, as he'd given up cold turkey about ten years earlier, in his mid-fifties. For forty years he'd smoke two packs a day of lung-busting Winfield Reds and then Winfield Blues, dropping from 16mg of tar to 12mg for 'health' reasons. Then one day he thought 'that's enough' and never smoked again. One day a heavy smoker, the next day not at all. Like some kind of superhuman freak. There are Buddhist monks who don't have that level of discipline. People spend years fighting their nicotine addictions with patches, hypnotherapy, tears. Ol' Ice Veins just thinks: I'm done. Decision made. End of story. Let's move on to the non-smoking chapter of my life.

Being a non-smoker – and apparently now the most chill person in the world – didn't mean Dad was suddenly a fun companion in a car. It just meant the trip was now less lung-cancery and shouty.

When I was a learner driver, Dad was deliberately the most annoying passenger possible. He tried to distract me at every opportunity. His rationale – like a fitness-obsessed coach taking his football team to high altitude – was that when I finally got into real conditions alone, I'd be more than prepared. Every lesson was a combination of him whistling, drumming, windows down, smoking, windows up, humming, opening and closing the glove box and constant radio station changes. I still can't believe we weren't involved in a fatality every time I was under his tutelage.

Not only was this an odd method, it was the complete opposite of what I'd observed as a backseat passenger when he was driving, when silence was a must for any long trip. Fights rarely kicked off in the back, and usually only happened when my sister was given a window seat. This is a privilege the youngest should never be granted, as everyone knows the last out of the womb gets the middle seat. Despite this breakdown of the social order, my sister would sit there, refusing to wind down her window. It was bad enough given the lack of air conditioning, but was made worse when it caused that weird painful thudding sensation in our ears, created by a change in air pressure only rear windows generate. That would set my brother and me into full over-the-top whinge mode, causing my sister to dig her heels in, which in turn set Dad off, who started yelling, 'If you kids don't stop mucking around I'll pull over! I'll pull over!'

We all knew it was an empty threat. No one was pulling over; no one was getting out. It's way too much effort. Though I like to think it did happen once and that's how Adelaide got started.

When I was a learner, Dad's approach wasn't necessary. I was already more than nervous enough about being in control of a two-tonne V8 weapon with balding tyres that handled like a yacht. The car was even more dangerous when it was raining – if you even slightly over-revved it on a wet surface, the back end would flick out and send you sideways across the road.

Whistling to distract the teenager in command of that death trap wasn't Dad's greatest idea. When we'd arrive home, Mum must've thought my through-the-roof excitement was at being allowed to drive, but it was actually a deep appreciation that I would live to see the next day.

As we drove out of Munich I was in control, but adamant Dad stay quiet. Perhaps I put it more bluntly, but it was as much for our safety as my sanity. Driving on the opposite side of the road might sound easy, but it requires constant concentration. It's as dangerous as trying to cut your own hair in the mirror.

All those years of Australian driving experiences were turned against me, habit making me look at the wrong side of the car, mirrors and road. As much as I tried to remind myself everything was opposite, split-second instinct took over, terrifyingly making me perform the exact opposite of what I intended. If you've ever driven a European car and indicated you were about to change lanes by switching on the windscreen wipers, you'll know what I mean. Once we'd settled onto the Autobahn, Dad couldn't help himself, whistling, drumming and fumbling around on the radio looking for the German equivalent of Gold FM (das Gold FM). He was a constant distraction, but this time I knew it wasn't calculated; he was relaxed and enjoying himself.

He thought the car was amazing. And he loved the smooth, flat surface we were allowed to do any speed on. Every time we drove by signs that warned motorists to slow down to 130km/h during inclement weather, his excitement rose. 'One-hundred-thirty kilometres an hour during a storm! Unbelievable!'

When I decided to wind us out to 180km/h and take a photo of the speedo, he surprisingly didn't have an issue with it. I expected to be told off for doing something so reckless, but not only did he not mind, he handed me the camera. This wasn't the man I had grown up with.

Except he definitely still was. He was the man who, every time the GPS gave a direction, pointed in that direction. Even after I told him to stop, he kept subtly doing it in his lap.

He was the man who, every time the GPS gave an instruction, would lean in to listen to her. He was nothing if not polite.

He was the man who, every five minutes, gave me a weather update, the temperature gauge in the car a new technology that had to be exploited.

Travelling at a speed of 'choose your own', we reached Bamberg, the town where he'd been born, in no time. I imagined for Dad it would be an odd feeling, returning to his place of birth some sixty-odd years after leaving. He didn't have any actual memories, but perhaps he would feel that deep connection I guess we all have with our hometown.

As we drove in through the outskirts of Bamberg, with all that weight of history and emotion, Dad had four words: 'Doesn't look very nice.'

BAMBERG

Dad's negativity at his first sight of Bamberg wasn't unexpected, but I was disappointed nonetheless. What I hated most was that being negative was a trait I'd picked up from him and had found hard to shake.

Though he wasn't like that in every situation. There would be times when he was *really* positive, particularly about me and the goings on in my life. The way he talked about my comedy career and what I should be doing felt like being at an Anthony Robbins seminar. But one where as well as building you up, the person running the seminar also pointed out the people currently on TV who he doesn't think are talented.

It was always a lottery which Dad I was going to get. If only to counter him, I needed to be positive, so I said, 'Give it a chance! What city looks good from the outskirts?'

I mean, that's why they're the outskirts. People don't care about the fringes. No one is painting up a factory in an industrial area in the hope of drawing tourists to it. Evaluating a town by its edges would be like getting judged when you first got up in the morning, wearing slightly soiled tracksuit pants tucked into your ugg boots. That's the outskirts. We were still a good distance from the heart of town, the bit that's had a shower and done its make-up.

Perhaps one day when another layer was added to the outside of the city and the outskirts became gentrified and easier on the eye, he might appreciate them. But by that time they'd be the innerskirts, and we'd be back home in Australia.

His reaction also confirmed that he'd done no research, and had no idea what to expect of Bamberg. I knew that it was a beautiful, world-heritage-listed town, and sure enough it lived up to the billing. It has a river running through its heart and is often referred to as Little Venice. That's because it's picturesque, not because it stinks and you're being ripped off at every turn by lame, overpriced gondola rides.

Having dealt with the ugliness of the city's outer layer, Dad and I found our accommodation, checked in, and for the first time headed out without any insider help from natives.

Striking out on our own in Bamberg was also be the first time I actually saw the necklace wallet Mum had demanded Dad buy before we left, designed to conceal a passport and other valuables. You know, valuables like the €2000 cash they pulled out before he left just in case Europe didn't have an ATM. Aside from ensuring Dad's identity remained safe from anyone willing to exploit it, all those wallets did was leave everyone in line behind him frustrated as he fumbled around under three layers of clothing, trying to retrieve the correct document.

Security had become paramount for Mum and Dad since I'd moved out. Whenever I visited, they were always behind a series of deadlocks and a security-mesh door, as though the house had been relocated to the Compton neighbourhood of Los Angeles. They were never that cautious while I was growing up, the front door only really being locked when we went to bed.

Dad never owned a wallet, his rationale being that a wallet alerted would-be thieves to the pocket that contained it, therefore making you a prime target for pickpocketing, a crime I'd never heard of being committed in all my time in Melbourne. It also ignored the fact he didn't actually having any credit cards for a pickpocket to drain, and he wasn't exactly a mafia don walking around with fat stacks of cash held together by rubber bands. Mostly because all his rubber bands were to be used for broken wrists.

It stood to reason that if Mum and Dad were worried about safety in their home city, their paranoia was going to be at peak levels when Dad left Australian shores. According to them, the news was always filled with stories about the horrible things that happened overseas. It was true, bad things did happen everywhere. That's life. But a nightly news bulletin is hardly going to run a story about eight tourists safely cycling through Colombia, having the time of their lives.

When I was in South America, Mum was in a state of high alert the entire time, only calling off my funeral once I'd landed back in Melbourne. By the time I flew to Afghanistan some years later, to entertain the Australian troops in Kabul, I knew not to tell her where I was headed. When I came back and told her where I'd been, seeing her bury her head in her hands told me it had been the right strategy.

The dangers of international travel are never helped by well-meaning people telling apocryphal (read: bullshit) stories. Like the time a friend of a friend was 'robbed by gypsies after a fake baby was thrown at her, which they caught, but then she discovered her purse was gone and hours later her bank accounts were drained, her house sold and her children forced into slavery, making iPhones during the day and Nikes at night. And they had to adopt the fake baby too. But they did like the Trevi Fountain.'

I myself had narrowly avoided trouble in Pisa, almost getting my backpack stolen after making the mistake of putting it down in a tourist hotspot. A move so stupid I may as well have just started handing the contents around to strangers. 'Just letting you know, you're going to need an adaptor for that Australian iPad charger!'

Fortunately I was travelling with a street-smart Argentinean who was wise to the world after, amongst other things, having a gun pulled on her at the camping store where she worked in Buenos Aires. When a couple of young guys sidled over to us on the pretence of asking for a cigarette, she happily obliged, distracting them while telling me in no uncertain terms to pick up my bag, which they'd been eyeing off. I'd had no idea.

Tourists are ripe for scams and theft, particularly if they're naive, inexperienced or the fucking idiot who walks around with a bumbag securely fastened with a flimsy plastic clip and a $10 000 camera loosely slung over their shoulder in classic 'please steal this immediately' fashion.

Just as Dad had been overly friendly at the outset of our journey, I had also been far too trusting on my first ever trip overseas. I stupidly assumed everyone had good intentions and wouldn't take advantage of me. Honestly, I don't think I even assumed people had any intentions at all, good or bad. I just didn't think about it. I'd never been duped so didn't even know it was a thing.

Upon my arrival in Amsterdam, when a man approached me and offered accommodation at a hostel, I immediately took it, thinking, 'How nice is this? They come right to the train station to help people out.'

I had no idea this guy was a long-term backpacker (already suspicious) working for a commission. Once I'd checked in he couldn't have given a shit that the hostel was located in a dodgy neighbourhood, the rooms were packed more tightly than Baghdad's Abu Ghraib prison and I was hustled playing pool in the hostel games room by the guy working the front desk. I lost some cash, learned my lesson and vowed to never again over-estimate my pool-playing abilities while so stoned I think I don't have hands.

Dad hadn't really been exposed to extreme poverty back home; we grew up in a middle-class neighbourhood, and home-lessness and poverty aren't rampant in Melbourne like they can be in other major cities. Perhaps homelessness is on the rise in the city, but he rarely goes there, so wouldn't see it aside from what's reported on the news.

As we wandered through the main plaza in Bamberg, my experience led me to instruct Dad to give back the religious card he'd just been handed by a homeless person. Dad had happily accepted this 'gift' with a smile and a genuine, 'Thanks a lot, mate.' Followed by utter disbelief when I told him he could only keep it if he paid for it. Which is what he was about to be asked to do.

He argued, 'But he gave it to me.' So I explained this was the MO for taking advantage of friendly tourists. They'd hand over the card and hope people would be too embarrassed to hand it back, preferring to fork over a small amount of money to avoid letting down a homeless person.

Handing it back with disdain, Dad was annoyed at the beggar, but also impressed with himself at being a part of an attempted scam, thus confirming his status as a proper tourist. He was even happier that I'd called out this grift without him losing any money. As we walked away, having dodged a €1 bullet,

Dad raised his inner alert status to Defcon Tom (the highest). Nothing would get through his defences from here on.

Heading over the main pedestrian bridge, into Bamberg's old town, the wheelchair beggar stood no chance. When he shook his tin at Dad, I thought, 'Good luck with that, mate. Unless you're offering cheap beer, you won't see a cent.' In Dad's eyes you had to earn your money, and sitting in a wheelchair rattling a tin wasn't going to cut it. Plus, what if the beggar didn't accept euros? No way Dad was going to risk being embarrassed like that.

As we reached the other side, I suggested we double back and get a photo for Mum of the two of us standing on the bridge over the river Regnitz. As we turned and started back, we saw the beggar get up out of his wheelchair and walk away. I thought nothing of it, but Dad's world was upended. Forget the pic for Mum – Dad wanted photographic evidence of this fraud unfolding right in front of him.

To say he was stunned is like saying the *Titanic* had a bit of a rough journey. Dad was personally affronted on behalf of anyone who had ever handed this man money on the assumption that he was restricted to his wheelchair. Dad's view was that if you're in a wheelchair, it had better be permanent, otherwise you do your begging from a regular chair. It was black and white for him: if you could walk at all, no wheelchair. The wheels were what made people cough up cash.

Dad was never big on handouts. He'd left school at fourteen to help make ends meet at home, and when he started his own family he worked extra jobs, as a barman and early mornings at the fruit markets, to help us get by. He thought relying on others was lazy. He couldn't believe it when I went on the dole, not when there were jobs all around that I could have taken. He was right, there were, but they weren't jobs that I wanted to do. I preferred the work the government made me do for the dole, i.e. pretending to look for a job. The *White Pages* didn't open themselves, old man.

Dad was born in post-war Bamberg in 1947, two years after his sister. It's always been curious to me that she was born in 1945, right as Germany started to collapse, a seemingly odd time to have sex. Unless of course my grandparents were really turned on by explosions and the approaching Red Army.

In 1949 they left it all behind, emigrating to Australia for a better life as Germany attempted to rebuild. I can't even imagine changing footy teams, so can't comprehend what it would be like picking up your life and moving it to the other side of the world. Though I guess when you've just lost your second world war in thirty years, there isn't a lot of hope for the future.

I never knew my grandfather, Roland, and on the rare occasion he was spoken about it was in hushed tones. While always stoic about the effect it had on him, it was clear Dad had zero respect for a man who walked out on his family.

I'd learned that in their early years in Australia, during Dad's childhood, his family basically tried to assimilate as quickly as they could. They didn't want to stand out. As migrants from the country that had fought and lost a war against Australia and its allies, I could see why.

So they lived in what they saw as the typical Australian way. Which, having been to Germany myself, probably didn't seem that far removed from their familiar lifestyle and customs. The only time my grandmother got caught out was when she was invited to a social gathering and was instructed to 'bring a plate'. If you'd grown up in Australia, you knew that 'a plate' contained goodies of your making – scones, lamingtons, honey joys, et al. My grandmother, new to Australia and its customs, did what she'd been asked and brought a plate – an empty one.

The next morning, I found myself sitting in the reception area of the Bamberg Municipal Archives. This was not high on my bucket list. The New York Department of Records, sure. Maybe even the Fitzroy Town Hall at a pinch. But not the Bamberg Municipal Archives.

We were there because Dad had managed to proudly drop into conversation with everyone we came into contact with that he was born in Bamberg. 'Yes, I would like another beer, and did I mention that even though I have an Australian accent, I was born here?' But only with the English-speaking staff; he hadn't remembered how to say all that in German.

Whenever he took a break from telling me how great the breakfast of coldcut meats and cheese was, he was chatting with the hotel manager, skilfully transitioning from how much he liked the beautiful rooms to explaining where he was born. He must've had her cornered for a while, because he managed to drop into their chat that his mum's surname was Krug. Turns out, it's quite a common name.

Turns out – even better – Krug is the name of a very popular beer made in Bavaria. We were in Bavaria. My mind instantly skipped to me being the heir to a German brewing company. It made sense: I do something good for Dad and the world repays me with beer. I could already see myself wearing lederhosen as I declared open the following year's Oktoberfest.

The hotel manager wrote down the address for the archives off the top of her head, as though assisting people searching for their family history was a regular occurrence. And strangely Dad was keen to go. For someone who only four days earlier had never shown any interest in family history, he sure was going to a lot of effort to find out about it.

Armed with information assembled back at home and the intel picked up at the family afternoon tea a few days earlier, we sat in the archives' foyer, waiting. If Dad was feeling any sense of anticipation here, he was going with standard operating procedure and showing none of it. He could either be waiting for his entire family history, leading to hundreds of new relatives, or for a haircut. Actually, there'd be more excitement about the haircut – no one wants long hair. It's 'not right on men'.

The wait wasn't long before we were called in to sit with the director of the archives, Dr Robert Zink. We sat and told our story, Dad passing on all the information he'd gathered, which was mostly hearsay and anecdotal, as few documents had survived the move to Australia.

Despite handing over all available information, Dad was disappointed the answers we were after didn't immediately come to hand. For my part, I instantly jumped to the conclusion that this didn't bode well. Bamberg is not a big town and Krug is a very common name, so it should have been easy to find some trace of our family. My conclusion was then usurped by a better, less pessimistic conclusion: that Krug is such a common name, it would take time to find the right Krugs.

Dr Zink explained that he couldn't help us in that moment, but the archive office would be in touch to let us know what they discovered. I took this to mean, 'You'll be forgotten before you have your second bratwurst for the day.' Which would be in about five minutes.

As we walked the hilly streets of Bamberg, Dad's physical struggles became obvious. He still said nothing, but was given away by a newly acquired limp. No matter how slowly I walked, he wasn't keeping up. I continued to play along, sitting and enjoying a beer for longer than usual.

I knew Dad was happy to rest because we ended up at an outdoor pub that had an unreasonable amount of wasps flying around, which would normally have had him scrambling. At one point I was up and out of my seat, standing away from our table until they flew on. I got my fear of them from Dad, but he was sitting tight, as it would have taken too much effort to get up. He would rather have suffered a swarm of stings than activate his knees.

Dinner was quieter than usual, Dad not really engaging in conversation beyond monosyllabic answers.

'What's going on, Tommy? Why are you so quiet? Not enough wasps in here?'

'I don't know . . .' he responded, trailing off. I was about to leave it there, but he followed it up with, 'Maybe I shouldn't have done this trip.'

I was shocked. I thought he wanted to be there. 'What do you mean?'

This was our chance. We could finally talk through it all. Maybe I could finally get him to open up about his family, his father abandoning him. It might even bring us closer together.

'Nah, nothing. Don't worry about it.'

And we were done. Plus a perfect score from the judges for an immaculately executed Typical Rozenbachs Response (TRR™).

But I was still confused. Did he mean he didn't want to be here with me? I knew I walked fast, but surely I'd been a pretty good travel companion so far. I wasn't the one throwing talc around like a Johnson & Johnson baron. Did he mean Bamberg specifically? Perhaps things hadn't improved for him even after we'd moved through the outskirts. Or was he homesick already, after only four days? He'd never been away from Mum this long, that was true. Or could it have been because he'd had no luck finding the roots of his family? If I'd gone this far and found nothing at all, I'd probably feel depressed too.

So many questions, with absolutely and utterly no way possible of finding out any answers. Beyond of course talking in a meaningful way with Dad, which was not about to happen. But I could see that a hug was in order, to show Dad that I cared for him and appreciated what he was going through. So I stood up, took a deep breath, and walked straight past him to the bar to order a couple of beers.

With a couple of drinks in him Dad was back to his old self, the reflection gone. We spoke of eventually getting back home to Melbourne, and he told me aside from looking forward to getting back into his routine, he was more excited about a primary school reunion happening a few weeks after we were due back.

'The girl who I saved from drowning will probably be there,' he casually dropped in.

I was shocked. Who goes to a primary school reunion? High school I understand – we all shared some pretty amazing times on our journeys into adulthood. But in primary school there were way too many pants-wetting incidents for anyone to want to relive that time.

More importantly, I guess . . . he had saved someone from drowning? Talk about burying the lede. For my whole life.

How had he never mentioned this before? Even if you stretch it out and say Dad saved her in his final year of primary school, when he was around twelve years old, that meant he'd sat on that story for over fifty years. It was even more annoying to know that he had the ability to be quiet for at least half a century, yet couldn't help himself when we were in the car and he saw a wind farm in a distant paddock and called out, 'Look, fan.'

If I was in his position, I'd be bringing it up at every available opportunity. Any time I went near a body of water I'd casually drop a 'saved someone from drowning once'.

When the swimming was on during the Olympics: 'That's a really impressive time and you need to be careful around pools; easy place to drown, which I saved someone from doing.'

No moment would be safe. 'Did someone say dessert? Can you drown it in chocolate sauce? Which is what the girl I saved didn't do.'

I'd have a range of merchandise publicising the fact. T-shirts, stubby holders, floaties. I'm sick of people not claiming their hero status. If a journalist asked me if I thought I was a hero for saving someone who was drowning, I'd be more than emphatic. 'YES! Now where's my key to the city?' I wouldn't be a shy hero.

From there on in I'd want to be known as 'Adam Rozenbachs: drowning preventer'.

Dad had been at his school swimming sports and noticed a girl at the bottom of the pool. Rather than running to get help, as most kids would have done, he just jumped in and pulled her to safety. I couldn't believe he had the wherewithal as a kid to do that.

Our primary school experiences couldn't have been more opposite. I'd suffered a similarly traumatic experience, even though it was largely my own fault.

The walk to prep that day was a normal one, Mum dropping me off at the gate and continuing on with my sister to her kindergarten. As my friend Stephen approached, I walked ahead to greet him, ensuring I was out of earshot of Mum when I told him I had the matches.

That morning I'd risen earlier than everyone and gone to the kitchen and stolen a box of Redheads. They were readily available and, with two smokers in the house, unlikely to be missed. Looking back, it's clear that what we did was premeditated, although I can't recall us planning any of it.

As the bell rang for the first break of the day – little play – four of us made a beeline for the toilet block, cramming into one cubicle together. I can't remember if it was voted upon, but I assume because I had been the one to bring them, I was the man chosen to strike the match. It took a few attempts as I'd never lit one before, but I'd seen it done often enough to understand the basic principle. Dad lit his matches by striking them towards his face, which was way cooler than the normal and safer strike away from the body. It also had the inherent danger and coolness of a burning match flying off into his face.

I managed to get one started and held it under the roll of toilet paper hanging by the toilet. I made a rookie mistake, holding it too close and under the concentrated part of the roll, so while it smoked a little, the paper didn't catch. Before long the match burned close to my fingers and I dropped it to the concrete floor.

Lighting another one, I made a point of holding it under the loose sheets that dangled from the roll, and that time it went up successfully. There was excitement in the cubicle but, to our dismay, we could hear even more from outside the cubicle. We hadn't shut the door behind us and law-breaking like that was always going to bring a crowd. But where there's an audience, there's a dobber, the words 'I'm telling Miss Monahan' enough to force us to abort our mission. Not that I could tell you, even now, what our mission was.

We blew out the flames and bolted from the toilets, trying to blend in with the non-arsonist members of this junior society as casually as we could.

As little play ended we lined up outside the classroom. We could tell from the over-exuberant chatter that word of our deeds had spread. It was only a matter of time before the law caught up with us.

I pressed the matches into someone else's hand and quickly moved away before they realised what had happened, hoping that with no evidence on me I might be able to talk my way out of it. But before we'd even walked back into the classroom, I was fingered as a co-conspirator, five-year-olds not known for their ability to stand up in the face of pressure. The Firesome Four, as we were soon named (only by me), were made to sit apart in the corners of the classroom, unable to talk to each other and get our stories straight.

It was both cool and terrifying that everyone knew we were in so much trouble. Cool because you couldn't buy that sort of reputation, and terrifying because I assumed I'd be dead before nightfall.

As we stood in the vice-principal's office, I knew we'd created a bad situation for ourselves, but even at that age I also understood it was not bad enough to warrant a dressing down from the top dog.

We'd tried to set fire to toilet paper in a wooden toilet block; if the fire had taken hold, the whole block would have gone up in flames within minutes, ensuring an expulsion for us and the best day of every other kid's life when the fire engines turned up. If that's not the principal's jurisdiction, I don't know what is.

The vice-principal's belt smashing down onto his desk tore me from that thought. I had never seen rage like that; not even in Dad when the bird threw the nectarine through our neighbour's window.

The belt to the desk was as bad as it got. We were yelled at, but not struck, and then marched back to our classroom, the rest of the day a blur as I waited for the inevitable. When Mum picked me up, I must've seemed like I had the world on my shoulders, waiting to get in the most trouble any young man had ever seen. Nothing came. That wasn't totally unexpected; she'd hand this one over to the old man.

I was in my bedroom when Dad got home, pretending to clean under my bed in case I had to live out my days under there. He came into the house, asked about dinner, kept chatting to Mum. Then he asked where I was. I took this as the summoning to my execution and slowly made my way out, wondering how it would all end. Could I get smacked to death? Would I be permanently banned from dinner and starve? Or perhaps an ironic fire-based punishment I'd not even considered.

But nothing came. Dad was just asking about my day. Nothing later that night. Not the next day. I ticked off each moment of potential punishment. Not parent–teacher night. Not on my last day of prep, nor my first day of grade one. The consequences of trying to set fire to the toilet block never came and I never spoke of it. Nothing happened to the other boys either. For the rest of my childhood I was too scared to mention it, even to the closest of friends, lest word leaked out and a retroactive punishment kicked in. Though I am expecting a disappointed call from Mum the moment she reaches this section.

It was time for us to head for Berlin, meaning Dad would be leaving his birthplace for the last time ever (unless his life took a seriously wild turn). He embraced the gravity of the moment exactly as you would have expected, by not acknowledging it for a second.

Once we were on the road, Dad chose not to use his monk-like ability to be silent for decades, which I now knew he possessed. Instead he happily pointed out the 'bloody fantastic' Autobahn surface every five minutes, in case I had forgotten or moved on. Every roadside sign, he would read out loud, 'Berlin!' Like living next to a train line and becoming oblivious to passing trains, he became white noise to me, constant but largely unnoticed.

The monotony only broke whenever we'd pass the golden arches, Dad getting audibly upset, groaning, 'Bloody McDonald's!' I'm not sure why it hurt it him so deeply, aggrieved by its very existence. Surely he would have gotten used to its presence driving around Melbourne. Maybe there was a cold Filet-o-Fish in 1973 he had never recovered from.

It would explain why I could count our childhood trips to McDonald's in one McNuggets six-pack; Dad ignoring our pleas, which went from when we saw the golden arches appear in the distance until they faded in the rear windscreen.

Fast food was crap; end of story.

Unless it was pizza. Or fish and chips.

BERLIN

My experience of staying in Airbnbs had always been great. The first few times were odd, going through the drawers of a stranger's house, like a burglar who was paying to be there. It was rare that I stayed somewhere while the owner was home, and once, in a basement in Seattle, I felt like I was in a seventies sitcom and my parents were upstairs. I did have my own entrance, but it made me feel like I was living at home and I vowed never to do that again. Generally, however, I enjoyed the comfort and warmth Airbnbs provided, making it feel like I was staying in my own place. A functioning kitchen was also really convenient.

The downsides were that complaints were much less direct, since you had to wait for the host or Airbnb itself to get back to you. Also, if you made a mess, the room wasn't reset during the day like in a hotel. No housekeeping meant no one replacing the soaps I didn't use or tucking the sheets in so tight I had to unmake the bed before I could get in. As I was fast discovering, it also meant no one sweeping up the talcum powder in the bathroom.

And, as was the case with our accommodation in Berlin's Prenzlauer Berg, no lifts. Which meant when we arrived, we had to carry our luggage up three flights of stairs. *That* suitcase of Dad's, up three flights of stairs. It was a struggle for both of us, Dad at the rear, pushing, me at the front, pulling, in constant fear of tumbling back down over the suitcase and Dad if I lost my footing or overbalanced.

When we finally got inside, I needed to see what else was in his suitcase, because every jumper he'd ever owned couldn't weigh that much. Strangely, I saw that he'd packed a roll of gaffer tape. You know, the tape mostly used by roadies and kidnappers. I wasn't entirely sure what he had planned, but considering we'd come this far, I supposed I was in.

But before I could ask him about the tape, Dad had become fascinated by the windows in the apartment. They had this particular type of window in a lot of the places we stayed in Europe that operated on a hinge system I'd never seen before. They're confusing to describe, so stick with me.

Known as 'tilt and turn windows', the key is that they have two sets of hinges – one set on the side and another on the bottom. The window is operated by a handle, not unlike a door handle. When the window's shut and locked, the handle points down. If you turn the handle 90 degrees, so it's parallel to the floor, the hinges on the side engage and the window opens horizontally, swinging all the way into the room. But if you turn the handle 180 degrees, until points skyward, the other hinges are engaged and the window opens vertically, making a small opening at the top.

I know, thrilling stuff. Before this, hinges had been an invisible part of life I rarely considered, like electricity or waiters. But of course Dad was obsessed by them. From here on, in every apartment we entered, he'd rush to the window, trying every hinge configuration, while I stood watching him and wondered if adult-onset autism was a thing.

He'd excitedly move the handle into every orientation, marvelling, 'Wow, look at this. Bloody amazing! I have to tell Jason about these!' As though my brother would share this love of hinges. As a carpenter, he'd no doubt *appreciate* them, but he'd be just as bemused by Dad's excitement as I was.

Being in such close proximity to Dad made me see for the first time that he was obsessive compulsive. In Berlin I also found him mucking about with the sink in our apartment to check out the water pressure. He pointed to the running water, making the ridiculous assumption I cared, to inform me, 'That's bloody good water pressure that.'

Growing up I'd either laughed off his idiosyncrasies or, more to the point, not even noticed them. I was probably too focused on trying to get my acne-ridden face through high school, which was a day-to-day prospect, wrestling with hormones and hierarchy. The only thing I paid attention to were which girls were wearing bras (most of them) and which girls were ignoring me (all of them).

Looking back, our house was always in order, way neater than all of my friends' places. Having grown up with it, I didn't know anything different. The surgical cleanliness of the kitchen after dinner seemed normal to me. Dad would start the washing up while we were still eating, then stand over us waiting for the last mouthful to be eaten, swiping the fork from our hands as we chewed it down. Trying to tell him to calm down through a mouthful of food, he'd reply, 'You don't need it anymore.'

Nothing was missed when Dad undertook something. He did all the household ironing himself, including underwear. For a long, long time I assumed pressed underpants were common-place. He also ironed Jason's work overalls. My brother would always be on the lookout for them coming in off the line, as fights would ensue if Dad got to them first and ironed them. No first-year apprentice wants to turn up to a building site with razor-sharp lines down the front of his overalls. I imagined him on the bus, desperately crumpling his kit, hoping that he'd sufficiently dulled the crease before his workmates spotted him.

Dad mowed our lawns without the grass catcher attached to the mower, even though we had one. Raking up all the clip-pings created hours of extra work, but he defended the practice by saying it produced a neater finish. The yard always looked good, but at the cost of so much extra work. In my mind, corners were made to be cut.

He always made sure to finish what he started. When we had bookshelves installed in the loungeroom, Dad stayed up all night to stain them. The only thing you should stay up all night to stain is your liver.

The only time he didn't follow through on something was when, hungover one Boxing Day, he knocked down part of the wall separating the loungeroom from the kitchen. He'd decided on a whim (and without consulting Mum) that he'd had enough of walking through two doors to get from one room to the other, so he created a shorter route. Much to Mum's anger, it remained a rectangular hole in the wall with no frame for a couple of years. It seemed unlike Dad to leave something unfinished, but in his mind the job was to make an easier path from the loungeroom to the kitchen, which he clearly considered he'd accomplished.

Until the trip I'd largely forgotten about this kind of behaviour. Now that I'd had a reminder, I used the downtime waiting at stations and airports to reflect on my conduct, living in fear I had taken on more of Dad's habits than I'd realised.

One thing that quickly came to mind was when, having just turned nineteen, Dad suggested I start wearing 'smart' jumpers. Knitted numbers with a crew neck that you might see on an 1800s sailor, or at a dad convention. His rationale being that I was a proper adult now and perhaps it was time to dress like one, rather than wearing T-shirts and hoodies all the time. Happy with my look but thinking maybe he knew what he was talking about, I went against my better judgement. Close friends laughing at my outfit showed me how good my judgement actually was.

But clothing was easy to change; I could take off a jumper, untuck a shirt. Reforming your personality and beliefs takes a lot more work. How do you fix something when you don't even know it's a problem? Ideally I'd be an amalgamation of the good parts of my parents, with none of the bad. But as I got older I was realising their traits had become mine, like a cocky repeating its owner. I've found myself saying to work colleagues, 'You should buy property; that never loses money.' Even though it absolutely does, and I know it. But I've heard it said so many times that it's ingrained deep in my psyche.

The first thing I'd noticed was my obsession with the Bureau of Meteorology rain radar when storms are about, though I'd say most people do that. But the day that I timed my washing machine's wash cycle, due to me not believing the countdown displayed on the machine was accurate (it wasn't), was the day I sadly knew I couldn't fight becoming him.

My fear was that perhaps, living alone, I was doing lots of things like Dad but didn't have anyone to point it out to me. Was it weird to have a rain gauge attached to my home-brew kit, itself powered by my home-built windmill? I guess I'll never know.

———

As we sat at the breakfast table on our first full day in Berlin, Dad enjoyed a coffee while I worked out our itinerary. Trying to get my bearings while looking at a map, I wondered aloud which way was north.

Dad said decisively, 'It's that way.'

Certain it wasn't in the direction his finger was pointing, but needing to know what made him so confident, I said, 'Yeah, I don't think it is. What makes you say that?'

'Well that's what I'd say if I was in Australia.'

I can confidently say this was the most flawed logic I'd ever encountered. I was glad we were in a big city where knowing directions wasn't critical. Had Dad and I been lost in the desert, desperate for water, knowing death was imminent, I wouldn't want to hear, 'I think there's water over there, because that's where the kitchen is at home.'

I was used to these 'Dad facts', having heard them all my life. He always said them with such conviction, as though suggesting you were naive if you didn't buy them. They were mostly harmless falsehoods, like everyone wears steel-capped workboots on their paper round, until I was called up for jury duty and he told me, for a task as important as that, I had to wear a suit. 'You're doing your civic duty. You can't look like a bum.'

Only when I surveyed the rest of the jury pool, decked out like I was heading to the Birdcage section at the Melbourne Cup, did it dawn on me that Dad had no idea what he was talking about. I didn't need a suit; I would've looked more at home in a tracksuit. Yet again I'd fallen for the advice of someone who had no idea what he was talking about. He acted like he was Wikipedia, but he was full of shit. So . . . Wikipedia.

Berlin's Checkpoint Charlie museum was one of the few things Dad had shown genuine interest in this entire trip. When I listed a few things for us to check out in Berlin, he didn't respond with 'What's that?' but rather 'Oh yeah, that sounds good.' I was pleased he was talking about it, thinking that we might finally start coming across tourist attractions he would be enthusiastic about.

Checkpoint Charlie had been one of the few crossings from West to East Berlin, a narrow street guarded by barricades, barbed wire and tanks. It was a storied place, the physical embodiment of the Cold War, capturing all the paranoia and tension between the West and the USSR. What Dad really wanted to see there was a car.

Dad was amazed at how East Germans had managed to smuggle people into the West in a space hollowed out in the guard of this car, next to the engine and above the front wheel. I'm sure they tried just hiding under a blanket on the back seat, but aside from being easily caught and subsequently executed, it would have made for a less exciting exhibit.

While we'd avoided the summer tourist crowds, our visit to Checkpoint Charlie fell on a Saturday, meaning it was packed. Tourists, families, communists lamenting better days, all fighting their way through the controlled mayhem. As we stood outside the entrance, Dad and I agreed that in case we (he) became separated/lost we'd meet at the guards' hut that still stood out front.

Knowing exactly what kind of tourists are out there, the Checkpoint Charlie museum had idiot-proofed itself with arrows on the floor indicating which way to travel through the exhibits, which kept the flow moving and manageable, like a historical Ikea. As we walked through we saw the progress of the wall until its eventual fall in 1989 and exhibits of what life was like in both East and West Berlin. Then we came to the exciting section: escape attempts.

As we moved through, I spotted the car and began heading towards it. I stopped as I reached it, but Dad was caught up in the crowd and was swept away from me, caught in a riptide of sightseers. Even though there were arrows on the floor, I was willing to be one of *those* tourists, ignoring the rules, because I knew how much Dad wanted to see the car. Lowering myself to the level of Australian-overseas-in-a-Collingwood-jumper, I drew attention to myself, yelling over everyone, 'Tommy! Over here! It's the car!'

By this stage Dad was about 4 metres away, the distance growing, but if he'd tried hard enough he could have hassled his way back through the crowd. One advantage to the Saturday visit was a lot of the visitors were kids, who could be easily be moved past (shoved out of the way).

Dad didn't bother with any of that. He waved me off with a, 'Nah, it's alright. I've seen it on tele.'

Zen is not a word anyone has ever associated with me. I regularly throw golf clubs (on the course; I'm not a psycho tossing four irons in the street). As a kid I was hosed down by Mum after disagreeing with my brother over an LBW decision a little too passionately while playing backyard cricket. All my life I had allowed frustrating moments to get the better of me.

In that moment at Checkpoint Charlie, every fibre of my being wanted that. Dad waving off the car and walking away churned my insides. I was ready to snap.

As I moved past (shoved aside) the children in my way to catch up with Dad, I wondered why we were even at Checkpoint Charlie. If he couldn't be bothered looking at anything he'd already seen on television, then I struggled to see why we'd made the effort of coming halfway around the world. We could have watched a *Europe on DVD* box set.

As a child, if I'd said I wanted to see something and then waved it off when we got there, Dad would never have let me get away with it. He would have made me stand in front of that East German car until I knew the pressure of each individual tyre. I grew up under a regime of 'enjoy it, or else!', the best method of education.

Not for the first time, I wondered how other people managed to travel with their parents. My friend Jean-Paul travelled to Tokyo with his Dad and, as far as I could tell, they seemed to enjoy themselves. When the sumo wrestlers tossed the salt onto the mat before a fight, I don't believe his dad leaned in and asked, 'I wonder who cleans that?'

A colleague of mine drove all the way from Mongolia to Paris with his son, and I still can't work out how that was achieved without ending in a murder–suicide somewhere in Siberia.

I was being as flexible as I could, trying not to force Dad to do too much against his will, but it wasn't really working out. We'd been spending far too much time together – the only breaks I got were sleep, going for a run or to the gym, or taking a three-hour shower – but I didn't really have any other option. If I did my own thing then he'd simply stay in the apartment by himself, and I'd feel guilty for abandoning him. I was in a no-win situation, too guilty to take a break but desperately needing one.

The only way I managed all this was thanks to the ultimate ace up my sleeve: I'd been to Europe before. Instead of losing my mind and letting Dad know in no uncertain terms what I thought of his indifference, I managed to hold it all in by thinking, 'It doesn't matter. You've seen this. Don't let it get to you.'

So to anyone considering travelling with a parent, my tip for maintaining a reasonable level of sanity (not all, but some) is to complete the exact same trip three months before by yourself.

It will be an expensive way to go about it, but in the long run you'll save money on therapy.

I should have known Dad wasn't genuinely enthusiastic about the car. The only time he gets excited about anything is when there's a large portion of food in the offing. Otherwise he has a resting heart rate of one.

One day at Mum and Dad's I wandered into Dad's TV room, where I found a list in his handwriting. Curious, I started to read it, for a few seconds unsure what exactly I was looking at. About halfway down the list I worked out that they were film reviews. Dad had written them for movies my brother had downloaded for him, making it easier for Jason to properly curate the next batch.

Last Cab to Darwin – not bad
The Big Short – shit
Trumbo – slow
The Drop – slow/good
Moonwalkers – crap
Are You Here – crap/slow
Automata – trash
The Captive – slow/crap

These are actual reviews of hundreds of people's hard work summed up in one word, sometimes two, if extra detail might provide a better idea of the film. I imagine he stressed that Jason should avoid 'slow/crap' as best he could.

I wasn't familiar with any of these films, so couldn't vouch for the accuracy of the reviews, but what I took from it was that I'm glad Dad doesn't review comedy. That kind of brutal honesty would have comedians curled up in the corner, sobbing, devastated by a one-word summation: 'shit'. When I'd been at the un-fun end of a bad review, I did my best to read between the lines in the search for a positive, or at least find a few words that could be used out of context to portray positivity. Even the world's best spin doctor would struggle to come out a victor with nothing to work with except 'shit'.

After Checkpoint Charlie, we spent an hour at the Topography of Terror, an exhibition about the Nazis' secret police forces, located on the former site of the SS and Gestapo headquarters. As if we hadn't soaked up quite enough misery at Dachau and Checkpoint Charlie, the cruel history just kept coming, an old section of the Berlin Wall hosting the exhibits as you walked along. The horror was relentless.

Keeping up his theme of understatement, Dad summed up the whole regime with, 'Hitler was a real bastard.' Though he's normally described as a monster or paranoid schizo-phrenic (Hitler, not the old man), I couldn't disagree with Dad's take.

———

It was Berlin where, for probably the first time ever, Dad and I went for a walk without a destination. For as long as we'd known each other, there was always a destination. To the MCG to watch a grand final, where I witnessed my first ever streaker. To the car after I'd broken my arm running from the ticket inspector at a train station, Dad wanting to be mad but holding back because he could see how much pain I was in. Back to bed as a seven-year-old after I woke up screaming during a night terror, him patting my back and soothing this crazed child who must've scared the hell out of everyone in the house. We'd walked together thousands of times. But always somewhere.

No one back home would believe Dad and I were out . . . wandering. Like a happy couple content with nothing more than each other's company. If I'd asked him to go for a walk back home he would've suspected a trap, too suspicious to say yes. But I figured I could give him a break from learning history against his will by ambling through the Tiergarten park at a pace so slow we looked like we were doing the mannequin challenge.

The park is a massive expanse of lawns, meadows and forest, right in the heart of the city. As we strolled through this tranquil landscape, I was reminded that Dad is one of those people who think they'll stop existing if they aren't making noise. When we were in the car I could justifiably tell him to be quiet, under the pretence that our lives were at risk while I was driving on the wrong side of the road. But just walking around, I couldn't claim anything was about safety, so was forced to hold my tongue as Dad pointed out unspectacular things that I could already see.

'Ducks! Police! Tram!' he'd exclaim, like an adult toddler.

An adoddler. I was travelling with an adoddler.

Outwardly I ignored it, reasoning with myself that it would be mean to tell him to be quiet with no excuse, but my mind was in overdrive. I realised I had seen this inane behaviour at home: when Mum informed me my brother was getting a pool installed at his house, Dad had helpfully added, 'Swimming pool.' It's just that I wasn't there enough to see how common it was.

Pointing out things I could see wasn't hurting anyone, so I had to ask myself, 'Is it really such a big deal?' The answer was yes. Yes, it was a big deal. It was doing my fucking head in.

But I had a motive for keeping my cool regardless, going all the way back to when I was fourteen. It was 5.30 am on a cold July morning. I had snoozed my alarm for the second time, the heavy downpour having already woken me a good twenty minutes earlier. I knew I had to be up soon to do my newspaper round, but getting soaked doing it made it a tough sell.

'Adam?' It was Dad, whispering so as not to wake my brother.

'Yeah?'

'Come on, get up. I'll take you today.'

Those words were like winning the lottery. Dad was going to drive me around on my paper round, saving me from drowning on my bike.

Experience had taught me not just any rain got me that treatment. It had to be torrential enough to wake everyone during the night. A standard shower would've been seen as nothing more than an opportunity for me to harden up.

I thanked Dad from the bottom of my heart (not out loud, of course). It was early. It was cold. It was wet. That was a trifecta of shit. I'd still get wet running from house to house, Dad rolling the papers up and handing them to me through the car window, but it would cut the time of the round in half. It also had the added bonus that we'd get to hang out together, without my brother and sister.

I proudly took Dad on what I'd deemed the fastest route, trying to finish the job as quickly as possible so we could get back home for a coffee and a Milo (not in the same mug). That route included our street where, handing me a paper out of the window, Dad said, 'Hang on a sec,' and left it hanging in the rain. I stood there confused, not understanding why he was letting the paper get soaked. All was explained when he gestured with his eyes to the house we were at. We were at the house of a neighbour who was disliked because he acted like he owned the street, telling us off for kicking the footy on the street or when my brother's mates would park out the front of his house, even though he had a driveway and only one car.

A huge grin came over my face. This was an adult being shit to another adult! What a world! We both held the paper, like a baton in a relay race where the objective is to be a bit of an arsehole, until Dad deemed it sufficiently wet for this type of rain but not enough to get me in trouble. I delivered it, knowing the paper would have to be opened with an extremely deft touch or risk being ripped apart and rendered useless. I prayed for the latter of course.

Being a kid, I took these kind of favours for granted. That was my right. And sure, maybe I took advantage of Dad's generosity, spraying his bedroom window with the garden hose to trick him into thinking it was pouring with rain and getting up to help me. But what kid wouldn't?

But that's the reason I kept my mouth shut when, in the Tiergarten, he loudly pointed out a squirrel.

In isolation none of these incidents – if you could even call them that – were that bad, but they were death by a thousand cuts. If you wanted to update that torture, it would be modernised to 'parents for a thousand hours'. It would be extremely effective.

'Your punishment today is to be subjected to your father for one thousand hours.'

'Please don't. I beg of you.'

'In a modern art gallery.'

'NOOOOOOOOOOOOOOOOOOOO!'

Our choice for dinner was Metzer Eck, a family-run pub just up the road from our accommodation in Prenzlauer Berg.

I decided we should eat there after its very traditional menu had grabbed my attention during a run earlier that day. The wood-panelled walls and fireplace gave it a nice cosy feeling as Dad grabbed a table in the corner, and I headed to the bar for another look at the menu. Traditional in Germany clearly meant potato-based, as almost every dish came with fried potatoes.

I bought a couple of beers and sat down, asking what Dad wanted. I didn't really catch what he said, as it was what he *wasn't* ordering that I was interested in. I'd seen on the menu that homemade lard was offered as an appetiser. Normally pig fat wasn't a reason I'd choose to dine anywhere, but for years Dad had regaled the family with stories about his favourite childhood treat: teddy bear biscuits with lard. Enthusiasm building, he would detail how they'd lather the sweet biscuits in lard, indulging in the oily pork combined with the sweetness of the biscuit. It was a treat brought over from Germany that, surprisingly, didn't catch on.

Even as a kid I should have been dubious. If he ate it as often as he claimed, he would have been dead of a heart attack at age nine.

But now it was time for him to put his hog fat where his mouth was. After not hearing 'lard' in anything he'd said he was considering ordering, I pointed it out on the menu.

Pretending to think about it, he answered, 'Nah, don't feel like it.'

If I hadn't eaten something I loved in forty years, I'd be out in the kitchen, helping plate up. We both knew he'd been called out, that his years of bragging had been brutally exposed. But I let it go, not wanting to embarrass him.

I'd save that for when I was telling Mum about the trip.

A week into our journey, Dad was starting to feel the monotony of travelling. Figuring out what to do, where to eat, how to get around, calculating exchange rates, waiting for things to open. Nothing was automatic, as simple as getting in his car and following a daily routine. Usually another tedious travel challenge is trying to work out which of your clothes you can wear again, but it wasn't an issue as Dad had brought his full wardrobe.

Plus, we were running out of things to say to each other, as became clear when Dad started repeating stories. About his trip to Germany. At one point I had to say, 'You know the person in that story is me? And that it was two days ago?' I was starting to get an appreciation of how difficult it would be for parents to keep a child occupied during school holidays.

After the non-lardfest, we headed back to our place, where I checked my email. The day before I had asked our Airbnb host in Paris if our accommodation was still all good, only to get the confusing reply, 'Which one?'

I thought that was odd, wondering to myself, 'How many do you have?' I replied with the address for the apartment I'd booked and put the whole thing out of my mind, 100 per cent confident that absolutely no trouble could come from the fact that this person did not know which apartment we had booked.

What I needed was space. I resolved to tell Dad that I'd head out once he fell asleep, which would hopefully lessen my guilt about leaving him alone. I was about to tell him my plans, but he'd already passed out on the couch. I would have liked to think the trip was tiring him out, but falling asleep after dinner was pretty standard.

As I made my way onto the darkened streets of Berlin I realised that, for the first time on the trip, I would be alone for a whole evening. I liked Berlin; its mixture of old buildings and new, modern architecture made it feel very Melbourne. I felt safe, whether that was warranted or not. The city had a great energy as people enjoyed their Saturday night.

As a fan of heavy metal music, I figured if was going to be in a bar where I didn't speak the language, I might as well go somewhere where I'd enjoy the music. I ended up at Nuke Club, a metal nightclub a few train stations away. It was a nice escape to relax and not have to make small talk for a while. It was a fairly uneventful night, aside from hearing someone yell 'NEIN! NEIN! NEIN!' in an attempt to stop a Nazi skinhead from throwing a bottle of beer off the balcony where we stood. It didn't work, the bottle landing on the crowd below. Of all the

countries where I thought skinheads might have toned themselves down a bit it should have been this one, what with the
whole losing the war thing.

On my way to the club I had contemplated what I would do
if I met a nice Fräulein. I didn't think I could stay at someone
else's place, because Dad would have been trapped; he could have
left the apartment on his own, but I knew he would have stayed
until I returned. I figured if I met a girl I would sneak her into
my bedroom and try not to wake Dad by having very quiet sex.
Which is a difficult thing to do, mainly because I'm very good
at it.

The loud music, darkness and language barrier in the club
took care of that dilemma anyway. I made absolutely no noise as
I went to bed by myself.

The next morning, as we readied ourselves to head to the
airport for our Paris flight, I checked my email one last time
before we got going. We'd had a reply from the archives office
in Bamberg.

Dear Mr Rozenbachs!

*When you visited Bamberg, you spoke to us about your
ancestor Hans Thomas Krug (and his wife Lydia) and you gave
us the information, that he served in WW I and both lived in
the city of Bamberg.*

*We now checked all our files and repositories, but we could
not find a person of that name. We therefore assume, that Hans*

Thomas Krug did not live in the city of Bamberg, but proba-
bly in the county of Bamberg, i.e. in one of the villages around.
Unfortunately the municipal archives do not have any docu-
ments and information of people outside the city.

But maybe you can provide us with more information on
Hans Thomas Krug (registration form, document of baptism or
similar), which show, that he lived in Bamberg. In this case we
could try to do further research on him.

Respectfully

Robert Zink

Already struggling with the strain of the trip, such disap-
pointing news was probably not what Dad needed as he prepared
to leave Germany for the final time. Again.

PARIS

Arriving in Paris blew Dad's mind. Just not in the way I'd hoped.

On the crowded train from Orly airport to the centre of Paris, I didn't notice he'd gone quiet. I missed it because I was concentrating intently on getting us to the right Metro station. Alarm bells should have been ringing though, because there were hundreds of things he could have pointed out, like 'policeman with machine gun', yet he was staying uncharacteristically silent.

I thought I understood his response. The first time I saw cops with machine guns, on a train from Berlin to Prague, I was shocked too. It's such a heavy-handed display, usually reserved for the military or anyone in America.

Dad had never seen a machine gun. Dad had never seen a police officer with a machine gun. Dad had never been on a train in a city that required a police officer with a machine gun. I'm sure it had him thinking, 'What sort of unsafe, overpopulated, machine-gun-needing hell hole has Adam brought me to?'

The train was packed, feeling more like we were headed to the footy at the MCG on a Saturday afternoon. Except that it was midday on a Tuesday. Dad wasn't used to overcrowding; he drove everywhere, so catching public transport was rare. He lived in the suburbs and worked even further away from the city, so didn't generally have to deal with masses of people like this. When he did, it was fleeting. Melbourne's population sits at around 5 million, whereas Berlin and Munich were a comparatively small 3.5 million and 1.5 million. This had lulled him into a false sense that European cities were easy to handle. Paris's 11 million people had caught him unawares, not least because all of them seemed to be on our train.

Getting around a foreign city's transit system is daunting. It's an overload of colours, names, trying to work out which stations connect, buying the right passes, and for us, lugging around a caravan-sized suitcase.

After an hour of very quiet travel from the airport, we arrived at the Hôtel de Ville station in the Le Marais district. I'd been told by a friend who'd once lived there that this was the older, gothic-architectured section of Paris, and a cool neighbourhood to boot, so it would have a lot of good bars and clubs for us to not go to. It was more rustic than anywhere we'd been in Germany; it had a kind of lived-in feeling, like a well-worn couch. Berlin felt almost brand-new in comparison, and I suppose that was courtesy of Allied bombing. The streets in Paris instantly felt a lot busier, both on the roads and the footpaths as people scurried about their day.

Arriving at what I thought was our accommodation, we waited for our host to show up and let us in. And waited. And continued to wait. We stood out the front, checking out the Parisian sights on our street, a bakery and a boarded-up store. We couldn't even ease the boredom by reading the graffiti scrawled across the plywood.

When our wait drifted out to half an hour, I felt the doubt start to creep in. Were we even at the right place? Were there two Le Marais districts? Had Airbnb closed down overnight? Was this the right Paris? According to my initial email correspondence we had the correct street and number, but it only led us to two huge, solid steel gates. Behind which I assumed was our apartment. The longer we stood there the more my anxiety grew, my brain telling me I'd completely stuffed this up.

Dad wasn't saying 'don't worry about it' like he did with the satnav in Germany, which only added to my stress. I tried to console myself with the thought that if the apartment fell through, it wouldn't be that much of a disaster; we were hardly in the outer reaches of Patagonia, discovering the only motel in a tiny country town had been transformed into a craft brewery. We could find someone else.

Then Jose arrived, a young Spanish guy whose name I only remembered from the childhood joke about the Spanish firefighters Jose and Jos-B. Turned out Jose being over an hour late was the least of our problems. Naively, I'd expected him to speak English. But why should he? We were in France and he was Spanish; neither of those countries required English. This was on us.

Had I been a more diligent student it wouldn't have been a problem, but my Spanish was based on starting lessons on four separate occasions, then giving up each time after learning the numbers, how to ask where the toilet is and the all-important 'beer please'. My French was even less than that.

Through about three broken languages and excessive hand gestures, we managed to ascertain which apartment we were supposed to be staying in. This aroused pretty significant suspicions on my part, as I figured if it was his place he would more than likely know which one it was. Clearly we were dealing with the frontman for a bunch of apartments, not something I was used to with Airbnb. My previous experiences had been that the person letting the apartment was the person who owned it.

We also worked out that we were now waiting on someone else for the key, adding to the feeling we were being duped, because why didn't Jose have it? I'd never before heard of a pre-host, the person whose role is to stand around with confused tourists, smiling and shrugging at them until the actual host arrived.

Jose's blasé attitude didn't help ease the tension that was steadily building. The upside was that, once we worked out Jose couldn't speak English, Dad and I talked openly about what a dodgy situation this was. In case Jose had a basic grasp of English he wasn't letting us in on, I instructed Dad to talk quickly, making it harder for us to be understood.

Even though Dad didn't blame me for the situation we were in I certainly did, and as I was launching into my one hundredth apology, Key Man finally arrived. Dad stayed remarkably calm, mainly because Jose and Key Man were strangers to him and he didn't want to lose his cool in front of them. I knew what being ten minutes late could do to him, and this was now out to ninety.

Key Man seemed pretty casual about the whole thing, laughing with pre-host Jose, as though his lateness was routine and we had nothing to be concerned about. He happily took us through the iron gates and into a giant courtyard that led to our apartment, smiling, asking us what we thought of Paris so far. He didn't get a lot of joy from us.

In Berlin, staying on the third storey without a lift had led to a fair amount of commentary from Dad. Not necessarily complaining, but weighted remarks, the ones that come across as jokes but aren't as innocent as they first sound.

'Fucking lift would be nice,' he said to me (with his eyes), as we headed up the stairs in Paris.

As we rounded a very tight corner with the world's still-heaviest suitcase to head up a fourth flight of stairs, I couldn't help laughing out loud. This whole situation had become a farce; a ninety-minute wait followed by four flights of cramped stairs. I was hoping Dad would see the funny side of it when we sat down with a beer later.

Then the door to the apartment opened.

The overwhelming train ride followed by the annoying wait for the key were both forgotten in an instant. That was a positive. The downside was we were now dragging our suitcases into the single worst apartment I'd ever seen.

Dad was quiet, and I wasn't sure whether he was holding his tongue in front of the strangers or if he'd been reduced to a catatonic state. Sweat dripped down my temples, either from carrying the luggage up those stairs or sheer embarrassment at what I'd booked. I barely heard Key Man as he explained where everything was, staring in disbelief at what we were being shown. As he left I gathered my senses enough to ask for the wi-fi password, which he provided, and then I closed the door behind him.

I turned slowly to face Dad, finding out very quickly he was far from catatonic and had indeed just been holding his tongue. What he said to me isn't fit for print, but in short, my reply was, 'Yes Father, agreed, this isn't a very nice place.'

Dilapidated would probably sell the horror of the apartment short.

The front door opened straight into the kitchen, which contained a hotplate that wouldn't have looked out of place in a camping ground, covered in grime from a thousand barbecues and only ever rinsed off when teenage boys pissed on it.

The couch looked as though it had been picked up from the hard rubbish collection outside a Vinnies, the second-hand store having decided it was too rundown and dangerous to sell. It sat on a ceramic tiled floor that at one stage must've been the surface for a bowling-ball-dropping competition. Displaced tiles and random jagged edges meant footwear was not optional.

The only window in the place was in the lounge, overlooking the courtyard we had just waited out the front of. A shabby curtain/rag was pulled across it, barely hiding the pitiful amount of light getting in.

The bedrooms contained sheetless mattresses, which in a past life must have been used to soak up spilled colostomy bags. If the mattresses were sponges (which they technically were) I would've tossed them out long ago, but at least they were hygienic because there was no way bacteria would have been stupid enough to stay.

As the host left he said there'd be linen delivered later, the cleaners having forgotten to drop it off when they were there earlier. Which, from the looks of it, was 1987.

I'd stayed in worse places. There was a backpackers in Laos that had the shower in the toilet cubicle, a neat design choice I didn't discover until I picked up a soggy and unusable roll of toilet paper at a moment where I very much needed a dry roll of toilet paper. But I could safely say Dad had never stayed anywhere this bad. His experiences were his house, which he liked, or if he and Mum ever did travel in Australia, hotels.

This apartment had the feel of a half-house you would see in a warzone, and I wasn't sure if we were in the still-standing half or the rubble. Either way, the bomb had blown the sheets off the mattresses. I was surprised the people of Damascus hadn't offered to sponsor us.

'Let's go grab a beer.' I blindsided Dad with this offer, but I needed to get him out of the apartment so we could figure out what to do. We both knew it was shocking; soaking in all its disgusting features, both figuratively and literally, wasn't helping.

Fortunately our wait had meant the time had drifted into mid-afternoon, so we found an open bar, ordered a couple of beers and attempted to work out our next move. The quaint cobblestoned streets of Le Marais were going to have to wait.

I desperately searched online for a hotel to stay at, but nothing was available in the area or within our budget, though Dad was willing to expand it, which showed how desperate he'd become. But as it became more and more depressingly obvious we were going to be forced to stay for at least one of the four nights we'd booked, Dad began to sulk. His sense of humour deserted him, and he wasn't open to any topic of conversation other than the shocking accommodation.

I'd never seen behaviour like this in him, because at home he usually had some sort of control over every situation. Sitting around wallowing wasn't his style. When he ended up in intensive care because of a serious car accident, his pelvis shattered, arms broken and head trauma resulting in eye sockets as black as coal, he defied the doctors and was in rehab weeks before they thought he'd be.

Now, for the first time ever, he'd basically given up. He was homesick, miserable and probably blamed me for the terrible apartment. Why wouldn't he? I certainly did.

Dad was adamant we should leave Paris immediately. I was equally firm about staying, reasoning that once we got out of the apartment and started hitting the sights, it wouldn't be so bad.

Dad wouldn't let it drop. 'I'm serious, Adam, I think we should go.'

'We can't. For starters, we've only been here for three hours.'

'So?'

'So? So I'm not getting back to Australia and when people ask me, "How was Paris?" I'm saying, "I don't know, only popped in for the afternoon." It's not going to happen.'

Dad wasn't happy with my response, but I couldn't let his rashness dictate our plans. The day had exposed vulnerabilities in him I'd never seen, or even knew existed. He was sore, homesick, and he missed Mum. He wouldn't even be able to relax at the end of the day because the apartment was so unwelcoming.

In the past he would've carried on stoically, but he'd been worn down to the point of despair most travellers reach at one time or another. A stomach bug might take hold, leaving you drained in the bathroom, desperately wishing you could be sick in the comfort of your own toilet bowl at home. It's not a fun predicament to be in, and this was Dad's first exposure to the feeling. He desperately wanted to go home, but I couldn't let him do it.

There are times responsibility thrusts itself upon us. That's how heroes happen, like Dad saving someone from drowning; he didn't think about it, he just acted. Now it was my turn. I stepped up and took full control. Not just the logistics, but getting Dad through this emotionally. I had to use my instincts to make our remaining time as easy as possible. And enjoyable. I didn't want it to turn into a hostage situation.

Stepping up filled me with dread. I'm never the responsible one. Only weeks earlier I'd been fined for drinking on the train. After leaving one party and heading to another, I decided to take public transport. Turns out the public transit system is not as au fait with the 'traveller' as taxis are. Sometimes you just need a drink with you on a journey, in case – god forbid – you sober up.

The moment I sat in my seat, the protective services officer made a beeline for me, deciding a fine was in order. Which was fair enough. I knew it was illegal. Once again I'd flown too close to the sun and had my wings burned.

As the officer wrote out my fine, I absentmindedly took another sip of my drink, which drew his ire.

'Mate! What did I just tell you about drinking on the train?'

I didn't help myself when I responded, 'Can you fine me twice?'

Turns out he could.

———

Before the trip with Dad, the last time I'd been put in charge of someone else hadn't ended well. Most of my friends had kids, and they assumed because they were responsible enough to look after them, I would be equally responsible. Turns out my friends are fools.

Jess was one of my oldest friends (in terms of the length of our friendship; she's not 104). She was one of the first in our group of friends to have a baby. I was even asked to be Rory's godparent, a nominal title that didn't really mean much other than that I'd shown a keen interest in him when he was born.

The usual spin on being a godparent is that you are expected to take care of the child should his parents die. (Spoiler alert: they did not.) But when Rory got to about two-and-a-half years old, Jess asked me to babysit him for a night while she and her husband went to the theatre. Sensing my reluctance, she attempted to persuade me, saying, 'You'll be fine, it's just for the night.'

I reminded her of my track record. 'It's a lot of pressure. I can't even remember my passport; how am I supposed to remember his allergies?'

She countered with, 'Seriously, Adam, you can do it. What could go wrong?'

Hundreds of scenarios ran through my head, from losing him to me somehow pulling the fridge down on top of myself and choking on slowly defrosting stale ice cubes (I have a vivid imagination).

On the night, I followed Jess's instructions to the letter. I entertained Rory for a while (watched him draw), gave up trying to get him to brush his teeth after about forty seconds and finally gave him his bottle as we readied for bed.

Then I put him in his cot. As Jess said he would, Rory called out once I'd left him, summoning me back to the bedroom, where I was instructed to sit with him until he fell asleep. I waited until his eyes closed, then eagerly went back to the lounge to watch Foxtel, which I didn't have at home. Here I had access to channels I normally couldn't watch, in particular the modelling channel.

As I sat back down on the couch, Rory called out again, and we began what was clearly a nightly dance. This time he didn't realise I was determined to stick it out until he fell asleep. I sat beside the cot, just about able to make out his wide-open eyes in the semi darkness.

'Go to sleep, mate.'

I figured I'd be back out watching TV in three minutes, five at the most. It turned out that the kid had stronger mental fortitude than me. He lasted a good fifteen minutes, staring at me unnervingly as I tried to pretend he wasn't. I was starting to regret giving him a couple of pre-dinner Red Bulls.

But I had to prove that I could outlast a two-year-old. Eventually I did, something I was way too proud of.

Just as I was about to reacquaint myself with the models, my phone buzzed in my pocket. I stepped into the backyard, not wanting my conversation to wake Rory. I kept it short, in case he woke again and called out.

Ending the call, I grabbed the door handle. It wouldn't turn. I knew instantly that I was locked out, but refused to believe it. I tried turning the handle harder, which has never worked but I hoped might on this occasion. It only confirmed what I already knew.

Unable to get into the house, there was only one way of checking whether Rory was asleep or awake: getting on all fours and sticking my head through the doggy door. Continuing my luck, it was so low that I couldn't even reach up and open the door from the inside. Why couldn't they have had a bigger dog, rather than a now long-gone tiny one? On the upside, there was silence inside the house. At least Rory was asleep.

I stood back up and cased the joint, looking for an entry point into the house. It felt like being a burglar, but one whose only possible means of entry was 'completely unlocked door'. To my dismay the front door was locked, as were the two front windows. I wasn't sure exactly what I was expecting; this inner-city house wasn't going to have lax country security.

Walking around the place, the only window that looked at all accessible was the one into Rory's room. I knew that wasn't the way to go. And if I was going to break in and startle him awake, then I'd at least want to be in full clown costume so as to completely ruin him for life.

During my lap of the house, my friend Nat rang to hear how it was all going. Word of me babysitting had filtered through our friendship group, and I had the feeling Nat had been put up to inquire about my progress. I explained my situation in the hope that she might provide a solution, but had to hang up when I was met with howls of laughter.

Every scenario I came up with ended with something broken, possible police attendance and a screaming, traumatised child. I stood in the backyard, feeling utterly useless. At least I had my phone with me. As I pulled it out of my pocket, resigned to the fact that it was time to call the locksmith, I was startled by it ringing. It was Jess. I figured that via Nat, word had passed pretty quickly all around Melbourne, the theatre production pausing to tell Jess she needed to call home immediately.

I answered, reluctantly. 'Hey Jess.'

'Hi! How's it all going?' she asked. The positivity in her voice told me she didn't know what was going on. I saw this as my chance to play it cool. If I paid off Nat and broke into the house silently without traumatising her son, Jess would never know.

'He's good. I fed him and put him down about fifteen minutes ago.'

Then I was overcome with guilt. This was one of my best friends, and my godson was stuck inside. So I blurted out, through peak levels of embarrassment, 'And now I'm in the backyard and I've locked myself out.'

She paused briefly before answering, just long enough to send me through six or seven shame spirals. It doesn't matter if you've been a mum for only five minutes, you instantly gain the ability to leave a silence that can cut through anyone.

'It's alright,' she said. 'There's a key in the backyard.'

And that was it. She directed me to the key, staying on the phone while I got myself back in the house and checked on her (still sleeping) son. Basically she looked after him via idiot proxy.

Not surprisingly, no one ever asked me to babysit again. Not just within my friendship group – even people who have never heard the story have the smarts to not trust me with their newborns.

But in difficult circumstances in Paris, I found myself with an oldborn, and I had to take care of him.

So I stepped up. Instead of telling Dad to 'stop sooking', which is what fathers of his era would have done, I played it delicately. Name calling wasn't going to help us, having about as much effect as telling an angry person to calm down. I needed to be firm but fair.

'We're not leaving, so get over yourself!'

Am I a hero for taking command? Probably not to the general public, but within my family, I had a public holiday dedicated to me.

Dad didn't like my course of action but there was little he could do. Every time he pushed back he could see I wasn't going to budge, so he surrendered, for the good of our relationship. It wasn't worth getting into an argument about it every five minutes. And he wasn't a worldly enough traveller to just say, 'Meet you in London,' and head out on his own, so he had to begrudgingly stick it out with me. Though this came at a cost, because now Dad was gloomy, hardly talking and not much fun to hang out with.

Seeing Dad as vulnerable for the first time was the perfect moment for our first ever hug. I didn't risk it though; even though he was miserable, I was still fairly sure he had the strength to push me into the Seine.

I could tell how much events were weighing on Dad, because in all the commotion we'd forgotten to eat. A nuclear fallout cloud could have been raining down on Melbourne and Dad would still have found time to reheat last night's roast lamb (using the radiation from the nuclear bomb).

We hadn't eaten because from Berlin to Paris we'd flown with easyJet. For the first-time flyer, the lack of frills with budget airlines can prove a bit of a shock. Free checked baggage, people to assist you with check-in, allocated seating – these are luxuries for those who can afford the *fancy* airlines. If you want a good seat on a cheap flight in Europe, it's first in, best dressed, and get the fuck out of my way old lady.

When the hosties walked the aisle with the food and drinks trolley, Dad was stunned he would have to pay for the cheese and crackers he'd just been handed. As a man of principle, he refused, 'I'm not bloody paying for them!', figuring his ticket should have been his right to at least a small amount of processed cheese and three tiny crackers. Reluctantly he handed back the snack, leaving him with the feeling that everyone in Europe was handing out items only in order to rip people off.

It also meant by the time evening came around, he was suffering from Post-Traumatic Snack Disorder. I suggested we go to a restaurant and sort the situation out. But even though we were both hungry, Dad didn't want to stay on the streets of Paris any longer. We had travelled less than 150 metres from our accommodation, but he already disliked Paris so much he preferred going back to our cell. It didn't matter that we were surrounded by so much culture and history, nothing made a difference to Dad. Having already had to talk him into staying in the city at all, I realised dinner wasn't a battle worth fighting; Paris would have to wait.

As we entered the flat, I nearly electrocuted myself on an exposed wire on the light switch. I knew then that we'd be leaving this apartment early, either by choice or by death.

I turned the television on and told Dad not to touch anything. I strolled up the street to the supermarket and grabbed some beers, salami, cheese and bread rolls – the backpackers' banquet – while praying that Dad wouldn't be impaled on an exposed couch spring while I was gone.

As I shopped, I couldn't work out how I'd booked that property. We've all seen misleading photos when looking at properties online, using wide-angle lenses to make a room look bigger or having someone with dwarfism stand next to a bar fridge to give a false sense of size. But I'd never been deceived like I had with that Airbnb apartment. Either the photos had been severely photoshopped or I'd booked it after getting home at 4 am one night.

While Dad cooked (cutting rolls and adding cheese and salami), I started an online chat with Airbnb, to let them know our issues and hopefully get us a refund. Amazingly, amongst all the problems, poor wi-fi was not one of them. It was so strong and fast I could've downloaded all of the world's television in about half an hour.

Dad had been miserable, but once I started listing the apartment's faults, he sprang to life. Now it was game on, Dad relishing the opportunity to find more defects than the ones we'd unearthed right away.

'That's not a bloody dryer,' he cried, as I listed the clothes horse that was advertised as a 'dryer'.

Forensically combing every centimetre of the apartment searching for faults, Dad even pried up a loose tile from the floor, insisting I photograph it. The anonymous person at Airbnb was exceptionally helpful and as Dad headed into the bathroom to find more evidence I told him I was already fairly confident we'd be getting our money back.

'Adam! Look at this!' he yelled, letting me know there was something amiss with the toilet. As I stood up to walk in and have a look, he was getting more excited. 'The water's coming right to the edge of the bowl!'

I reached the door to see him standing precariously on tiptoe, transfixed by whether or not the water would go over the edge. It didn't, but he demanded I add it to the list.

It's a well-worn expression to be careful what you wish for, and from the moment we'd agreed to this trip I'd wished Dad would show some passion for anything we did. I could not have guessed it would be this apartment that would ignite something within him. Berlin Wall? It's a wall, sure, whatever. Clothes horse listed as a dryer? HE'S ALIVE!

The apartment was so bad, it probably didn't even have the hinges Dad liked. We didn't check, too scared to open the window in case it fell out of the wall and crushed someone in the courtyard four storeys below. No way Dad was going down that many flights of stairs to check on someone's health.

Having compiled a comprehensive list of the apartment's failings, I thought there'd probably be one more to add – I wasn't overly hopeful the fresh linen we were waiting on would be delivered by the time we were ready for bed (it wasn't). This wasn't hell, but if there was a place just outside of hell where Satan let his friends stay during the holidays, this was it.

The shambolic dealings with pre-host Jose and Key Man set the tone of Paris for Dad. He wasn't about to get fooled by anyone again. Those two untrustworthy men were why he didn't carry a wallet (unless it was a passport wallet). This was why he lived in suburban Melbourne and didn't venture beyond it. Anything could happen, and was probably about to. Paris had burned him and he wasn't about to forget.

I knew what I was up against. It's hard enough reversing your own opinion, let alone someone else's. Sometimes we not only judge a book by its cover, but buy a thousand copies of the book so we can burn it on a huge pile. But I had faith that if any city in the world could bring Dad around, it would be Paris. Why else would so many millions of people, including the Romans, go there and romanticise it? It must be doing something right.

By the time we finally ventured further than 150 metres from the apartment the next morning, Dad had seen enough to sum up the city of love. 'Smells like cat piss.'

The odour was just the beginning of his dislike for the city. Everything Dad saw reaffirmed his prejudices.

Dogs in shops.

Dogs shitting in the streets, with no one bothering to pick it up.

People shitting in the streets. Probably.

This was exactly the type of city he'd read about, or seen in the documentary *Paris Will Knife You in the Back and Dump Your Body in the Seine*.

I felt bad that he hated it so much, but his desire to leave was overridden by me not having been to Paris before. I wanted to actually see some of the sights. I took Dad's feelings into consideration, considerably trimming down the list of places we were planning to go.

First stop: the pièce de résistance of Paris's tourist attractions – if not the world's – the Eiffel Tower. I had faith it would win him over.

'Thought it would be bigger.'

Those were his words as we rounded a corner and the Eiffel Tower came into view.

I can't imagine what he was expecting. The Eureka Tower, Melbourne's tallest building, is 297 metres tall. On a worldwide scale, it's splashing around in the shallow end of the pool compared to some of the buildings in China or the Middle East, but it's a standout on the Melbourne skyline and Dad's not seen anything bigger in person.

The Eiffel Tower is *the same height*, even though it was built over a century earlier. I didn't know how he couldn't think it was impressive. Sure, it wasn't the most amazing thing ever built, but it's not like Dad had travelled the world comparing grand structures. Though he had seen a lot of things on television, so perhaps by his standards he had.

For some reason he was itching to move on, but considering I was his tour guide he was stuck until I said we could leave. Not that I was planning on milking it, but I wanted to stick around a bit longer than a single derogatory comment.

One of the activities available at the Eiffel Tower is to climb it. We both knew that wasn't going to happen – for a very good reason.

During summer holidays our family always ended up at the carnival in the seaside suburb of Dromana. Carnivals are supposed to be fun places for kids. Being young means you're blind to the fact that the rides are being assembled and operated by carnies, people who can barely look after their own teeth, let alone the safety of hundreds of people.

We'd hit the carnival with family friends, and there was always a split into two factions: one group of children wanted to go on all the rides, the other group wanted to remain on terra firma. I say the other group – it was only me and our friends' daughter, Rennae. Mum and Dad knew I was terrified of heights and wouldn't let me go on anything, for fear of the consequences. And as much as she wanted to be in the cool group, Rennae was only four years old, so she was relegated to Group Lame-o for safety reasons (by the parents – for the right price, the carnies would have let her operate the rides).

The fun group took off quickly, trying to get through as many rides as possible before closing. Rennae and I were left with the rides that were deemed safe. We quickly discovered what can only be described as the baby ferris wheel. Rennae was all for it, and Mum, after much consideration and convincing from me, decided it was small enough that I would be comfortable riding it.

We boarded, all smiles and excitement, which lasted approximately twelve seconds before I lost what can only be described as 'my shit'.

I've since learned to cope with heights – planes don't bother me, I've even sucked it up and nervously flown in helicopters – but on that day, any semblance of being brave in front of a four-year-old went out the window. It was pure, unadulterated hysteria, so full on it set Rennae off too. Now it was two screaming children aboard the Ferris Wheel of Death.

Credit where it's due, the carnies flew into action, stopping the ride immediately and beginning the rescue mission. On a normal ferris wheel, they'd have to wait for the ride to complete a full rotation to get someone off. Fortunately this one was so small, the carnie basically reached across and lifted me out, like taking a kid out of a particularly tall high chair, ending the most traumatic moment of my young life.

Deep down, I know that horrific (for me) and embarrassing (for Dad) memory was the reason neither of us wanted to climb the Eiffel Tower. We happily settled on the mutually agreed excuse that the line was way too long.

Dad remained eager to move on. He must have thought that if we got through the tourist attractions quickly, we'd be able to leave Paris earlier. He couldn't have been more wrong.

My motto for the whole trip was fast becoming, 'We're only here once, so . . .'

That was one of those moments. I didn't want him to glance at the Eiffel Tower, say something dismissive, and then walk away within two minutes. I wanted him to stand there, taking everything in. Admiring it. Appreciating that when it was built it was a great feat of engineering and construction. As touristy as it had become, I imagine as a Parisian it would have been pretty cool at an earlier, less busy time to be able to sit on the grass that surrounds it and look down to the river or read a book under one of the world's most iconic structures. Now it's anything but, with thousands of people trying to do that 'look like you're holding the Eiffel Tower between two fingers' picture or the hundreds of peddlers trying to sell dinky, cheap souvenirs.

I kept trying to draw his attention to the tower, but his mind was elsewhere. Standing at this beacon of hope for the occupied Parisians during World War II, Dad fired off a bunch of questions within a minute. I answered them as rapidly as they came. 'Yeah, there are a lot of those guys selling the miniature Eiffel Towers.' 'They probably *are* a rip-off. Who cares?' 'I don't know where they'd get that many.' 'Why should they be arrested?' 'How about you forget about them and look at the actual-sized tower right there?'

Eventually I managed to get his focus back to the tower and, as he stood there finally taking it in, Dad managed to give it some praise.

'That's good steel that.'

All of a sudden I was travelling with the head of Rio Tinto.

The Eiffel Tower summarily shut down by Dad, as though he was on an engineering Tinder date and would only accept 400-metre-plus structures, I wanted to give other famous Paris sites equal opportunity to disappoint him.

As we made our way up the stairs to the Sacré-Cœur church, I heard Dad mumbling to himself. I figured he was urging himself to go on, the pain of the climb becoming too much for him but refusing to quit.

I asked what he was saying, curious as to what mantra was helping him push through. By now, I should've known this was a dangerous strategy; I didn't really want to go back inside that head of his, but by this stage of the trip I was concerned about his welfare. Perhaps he genuinely was in we'd-better-stop-for-his-long-term-health kind of pain. His safe return to Mum weighed heavily on me, so I didn't really think of the consequences when I asked.

'I'm counting all the stairs we're going up.'

Sacré-Cœur will always stay with me for its look-at-me value. I could tell its architects had gone all out to impress, building it out of white stone, loading it up with five domes, a huge bell tower and massive columns on the portico leading to the entrance. On the top of a hill overlooking Paris. This church wanted to be noticed and they nailed it. The interior was just as impressive, incredible stained-glass windows casting people in various colours as a mural of Jesus watched over everyone.

For Dad, it will live on only as the number of steps he had to climb to get there.

To this day, Dad could still give a stair count for each of the major tourist attractions we went to. The numbers have never changed, filed away in the vault within his brain alongside the beggar who stood up out of his wheelchair and the great fish and chips he later ate in London.

He justified counting steps as helping take his mind off them, the constant up and down causing him angst. I completely understood. We've all been in a position where we need to dig deep to carry on, struggling through a run, mid-winter at work or season three of *Orange Is the New Black*. What couldn't be justified was his need to turn to me and say, 'twenty-seven,' every time we ascended a flight.

Or discussing it with me later. 'A hundred and eighty-two stairs! Bloody hell, that's a lot, isn't it?' is not the gateway to mean-ingful conversation. It's the gateway to the room in hell you never want to end up in: the Meaningless Dad Conversation Room. Where on a loop you'll hear about the weather, your brother's car, how footy's not as good as it used to be and the weather.

Even when I asked him directly, he still wasn't saying anything about the pain I knew he'd been in since Munich.

Short of telling him I'd eavesdropped on his conversation with Mum, and that I knew for a fact that the walking was hurting him, I didn't know what I could do to help him if he wouldn't admit it. Frustrating as his silence may have been, at the same time I was impressed by his not quitting. As a kid I was exceptionally prone to a good old-fashioned quit.

After a few schoolyard scuffles, Dad and I agreed (95/5 split his way) that I should take up some form of self-defence. He decided to teach me boxing, but this ended quickly, after he attempted to make a floor-to-ceiling speedball.

This consisted of a netball wrapped in a cloth masking tape attached to two occy straps, one rising to the ceiling and the other secured to a spare tyre on the ground. It almost worked, aside from the exceptionally rough tape used to secure the occy straps to the ball, which shredded my knuckles and cause them to bleed in an instant. If my bloodied and weeping hands weren't enough of a hindrance, the occy straps would regularly come away from the tape, or work their way off the tyre, the loose end snapping back at a speed that almost took my eye out. Although that taught me mongoose-like quickness, I gave up boxing because I didn't need the extra attention an eyepatch would bring me in the schoolyard.

Instead I chose tae kwon do, based on my love of martial arts (mostly from the TV series *Monkey Magic*) and the fact that our neighbours did it, giving me easy (free) access to uniforms. I figured a few roundhouse kicks would sort out any issues that came my way in the foreseeable future.

Lessons were paid for and off I went, gaining a yellow belt in relatively quick time. While this sounds like an achievement, gradings at that level were nothing more than a basic walk-through involving a couple of punches, a random kick or two, and some well-placed yelling.

Stepping up to the next level involved shadow sparring with more experienced kids in the class. During one such shadow spar – *shadow* being the operative word – an aforementioned round-house kick landed firmly in my stomach. A literal kick in the guts. Blows were not supposed to land (SHADOW!!!) at that stage of our development, and though it was an accident, I'm not convinced the ninja I was sparring couldn't have held back a little.

Seeing me go down, the instructor came over and asked what had happened. Hearing my explanation, he merely said, 'You should have tensed up.'

It was advice I should have taken on board, and would have, had I not already quit tae kwon do halfway to the ground.

Since then, I've gained a steely resolve at becoming the best quitter I can be. Spanish lessons, careers in IT and PT, drums, relationships – I've quit them all. The one thing I never quit was comedy. I've stuck with it through some truly horrible moments, including performing late at night to tiny crowds, dying an awful death, and being introduced as a ventriloquist then performing to bewildered people who couldn't work out why my lips were moving or why my puppet was invisible. There'd be flickers of hope, but on the whole the early years were a slog.

When I moved back home, jobless, struggling to make any money, even Dad openly questioned what I was doing – 'You're wasting your life!' – obviously worried about my future but not putting it particularly eloquently.

Comedy was something I loved, though, and the determination and stupid inflexibility I'd witnessed in Dad shone through. I gritted my teeth when all signs were pointing me in the direction of quitting.

The wheel eventually turned and comedy became a career. The more 'flying hours' I got on stage the more confident I became, which in turn led to more work, and eventually a job writing in television on *The Russell Gilbert Show*. I started to discover my voice on stage and my stand-up improved because of it. I knew who I was and looked forward to expressing it.

Dad became a regular at my shows, always asking when I was on. Mum still hasn't seen me perform, due to my choice of content and her long-held belief that 'you don't have to swear to be clever'.

I've never aimed to be clever.

Though I'm not overly sentimental, I would always try to grab a souvenir from each country I visited. A steel dragon paperweight from Laos, a chunk of Machu Picchu, an improvised explosive device from Afghanistan. They didn't have to be expensive or functional, but they were always nice reminders of a particular period in my life.

My favourite were Che Guevara brand cigarettes I bought in Peru. '¡Viva la nicotina!'

Fridge magnets are probably the easiest souvenir to grab, a cheap trinket that can be thrown in the suitcase, proving it's the I-grabbed-this-in-the-departure-lounge-at-the-airport-on-the-way-home thought that counts. The choices presented to you are often cheeky or quirky, like a penis-shaped bottle opener, or a tiny bottle of Champagne. In the shape of a penis.

Dad wasn't one to buy that sort of thing, or as he'd put it, 'Not wasting my bloody money.' Not even for Mum. He'd had his choice of a hundred mini Eiffel Towers if he so desired, but no, his choice of souvenir was something that wasn't for sale. And it was something that he hated.

Though stairs had become Dad's mortal enemy, they weren't the sole focus of his hatred. When he wasn't climbing steps, cobblestones were also wreaking havoc. Dad complained that he was constantly rolling his ankles and jarring his knees, which I found strange considering I was walking the same streets and hadn't even thought about them. I checked and he wasn't wearing high heels either. So they made his list, and if you've ever been to Europe, you'd know cobblestones are like Dave Hughes; they're everywhere.

Cobblestones are remnants of cities being built hundreds of years before concrete was readily available. In Australia, they're pretty much confined to inner-city laneways, but in Europe they're a staple of most streets. Dad hated them, mumbling, 'Oh, these bloody cobblestones,' as we made our way along them.

Occasionally his focus would shift to complaining about the stairs, but once we'd ascended/descended – and he'd given me the obligatory 'forty-eight', just in case this was the time I wanted to know – his mind would shift back to the pavers under foot.

Therefore, of course, it stood to reason that if he hated something so much he had to bring some home with him. It made no sense to me – I couldn't imagine Schapelle Corby bringing home a mattress from Bali's Kerobokan Prison – but that's what Dad did. He chose a cobblestone as his one souvenir from Europe.

It wasn't the familiar Australian-sized bluestone, but more the size and shape of a Rubik's cube that had let itself go a little. He picked it from a pile when we were walking past some road-works, as though he was plucking a ripe peach off a tree in an orchard. From the literally thousands of things that could serve as a reminder of our trip, he chose the one I'm almost certain no one has taken home before: unlaid street. As if Dad's suitcase hadn't been heavy enough, from Paris on it had the added weight of street paving.

Against all odds, we made it to a second full day in Paris. We woke to the news that Airbnb would give us a complete refund on the apartment, so Dad was happy. Having seen how miserable a time he was having, I told him we'd leave a day earlier than planned, making him even happier. Money back and leaving Paris – it was all coming up Tommy!

With a spring in our steps, we hit the streets of Paris once again. Only it was pouring with rain, and the heavily overcast sky told us this wasn't a passing shower. (Our apartment window faced into a roofed courtyard, so we'd had no idea.) It didn't have to be said out loud that this would be added to Tommy's Great List of Terrible Things about Paris. The upside was that at least it would wash away some of the cat piss.

We bought umbrellas, a new experience for Dad. He had a car, why would he need an umbrella? None of my childhood memories involved Dad and an umbrella. I'm not talking about anything extravagant, Dad twirling one as he skipped down the street enjoying a sun shower. Just using an umbrella. He never owned one because his theory was, 'Getting wet won't hurt you.'

Even at the footy, when it was bucketing down with rain, we didn't have an umbrella. Dad had access to rolls of thick plastic from work, like a super heavy-duty Glad Wrap, and would hand-cut human-sized sheets to drape over us, which actually did a pretty good job. Here his argument was that the humble umbrella wasn't up to the job. Apparently normal rain did not warrant any kind of protection at all, but once it got heavy, a custom-built solution was required. Which would explain why I was only ever offered help on the paper round once the storm had been given a name by the weather bureau. So while everyone around us dealt with umbrellas being turned inside out by high winds, or being told off because they were restricting the views of those behind them, we sat bone dry in our own personal bubbles.

Though Dad was never worried about water, he'd have a meltdown if we ever sat on cold concrete. According to him, this was a recipe for piles. In my entire lifetime I've never heard of a kid with piles. How cold does it have to be, and how long do you have to sit there, before piles becomes a thing? Even though I doubted its existence, I avoided sitting on cold concrete, because I lived in fear of missing out on my under-12s footy grand final, listed on the injury sheet as 'A. Rozenbachs: Piles.'

I tried to enjoy the scenery as we wandered around Paris, but was distracted by Dad's animosity towards the whole city. His sense of being overwhelmed when we arrived on the train had not dissipated. To him, Paris was in a constant state of peak hour. The roads were jammed and the footpaths never-endingly busy, keeping us both on our toes in case we bumped into someone racing somewhere else Dad wouldn't want to go.

The trains were always full too, not allowing Dad the respite a seat might have brought him. I'd have liked to slow down, to read a book in a café or sit in a bar with no intentions, but that wasn't something I could do with Dad. It wasn't his thing, and we were now constantly on the move, trying to tick things off so we could leave the city as soon as possible.

I still hoped that somehow his attitude might suddenly change against all odds, making him demand to hang around an extra day as he was overcome by the glory of Notre Dame. But when we arrived we saw the line to get into the 700-year-old cathedral was at least 200 metres long, and we both knew instantly there was no way we were going inside. The wait to simply buy an entry ticket would have been at least an hour, and Dad was already aware no one was giving up the names of the cleaners, so he wasn't about to be sucked in by that again. Instead we just stood around outside, half-heartedly admiring the gothic arches and meticulously detailed figures in the architecture. At least when the roof was destroyed by fire a few years later, we had the cherished memory of sort of seeing it from the outside before moving on.

When we reached the Louvre, Dad gave it a bit of, 'I'll go in if you want to.' My experience of the last few days had taught me that looking at old artwork with him would be a waste of time. If he thought the Eiffel Tower was rubbish, I don't think the world was ready for his take on the Mona Lisa. Which probably would have been: 'What's the frame made out of?'

As much as he hated it, Dad kept on trudging around through the pain. We walked along the Champs-Élysées, full of expensive touristy cafes and luxury stores we'd never go into. If I'd had more time, or less Dad, I would've liked to try and get off the beaten tourist track, to see what Paris truly had to offer that wasn't superficial and aimed at people just dropping in.

I wondered what it would have been like if we'd had a great apartment, if Dad might have enjoyed it a little more. I felt bad that he hated it. I'd dragged him there and he wasn't having fun, so I tried my best to keep his spirits up and our time there short.

Dad did surprise me by walking up to the terrace at the Arc de Triomphe. Perhaps my message of 'you're only here once' had sunk in, making him suck it up and check out the view. Or maybe it was only because the terrace gave him sweeping views of the city, so he could hate more of it at once. It also gave him a new set of stairs to complain about/count.

The driving rain and wet shoes eventually forced us off the streets earlier than I'd have liked, but Dad was happy to be back in our hellesque apartment. It meant it was time to pack, ready to leave Paris in the morning.

CAEN

For probably the first time in his life, the next morning Dad didn't bother to make the bed or clean up after himself. He couldn't get out of Paris fast enough. If the option had been available, he'd have lined up outside the car hire place at 5 am, like he was waiting for the latest Apple product to be released.

We were headed for Caen. Pronounced Cane. Or Cannes. Or Cairns. I could never get it right. It's a town about three hours west of Paris, in Normandy.

Even though we were on a sealed freeway and not really in the countryside, there were enough fields and meadows off to the side to let us know we were free of the city. A distinct lack of traffic helped too. Dad could finally relax. We hired a Renault, which wasn't anywhere near as luxurious as the Mercedes we'd hired in Germany. It wasn't said aloud, but I have no doubt the lack of heated seats made a list.

It seemed we were coming to a toll station every five minutes, and I had no idea how much I was being charged each time I fed my credit card into the slot. But Dad didn't complain about the tolls; they were barriers we were putting between us and the dreaded city we were leaving behind. Cost wasn't important anymore.

I'd put Normandy on our itinerary so I could see the beaches where the Allies made the famous D-Day landings of World War II, turning the tide of the war. If you're not familiar with D-Day, it's the opening battle scene of *Saving Private Ryan*. If you're not familiar with *Saving Private Ryan*, think *Beaches*, but with Bette Midler pinned on the beach by Wehrmacht machine-gun fire and then getting her arm blown off.

Driving out to Caen, to see a series of beaches Dad had zero interest in, I started to get the sense that I'd made a mistake by making the trip as long as I had. For me, time off was a precious resource, so whenever I travelled, I tried to maximise every waking moment. Particularly when it was Europe or South America, I felt I needed to stay as long as I could to justify how long it had taken me to get there from Australia. I'd already lost two days of holiday time flying there and back, so I wanted to make the most of the rest.

I usually timed my arrival home to be the day before I went back to work, not concerning myself with jetlag because I could recover on company time. Usually the writing assignments I worked on weren't expected to be completed in a day, so as long as I kept myself alert enough during meetings with Nō-Dōz washed down with coffees topped up with Red Bull, I could fudge my way through the day and make sure I was okay enough to get it all done the following day.

If I was staying at a resort, then ten days of holidays was plenty. Time doesn't matter when all you're doing is lying around a pool. The biggest issue I faced on those holidays was hoping no one noticed I'd spent four hours at the pool bar without getting out to go to the bathroom.

But somewhere like Europe, full of history and culture, plus all kinds of different regions and landscapes and cities, you want to go for as long as possible to take it all in. And for the unprepared, i.e. Dad, three weeks on the road can be a shock. Like dog years, Dad had his own sense of time – if you'd asked him in Caen, which was the two-week mark of our holiday, in Dad years we'd already been in Europe half his life. The excitement of Munich was long gone; he was bored now, just getting through each minute until we could get home. He didn't complain, resigned to the fact that we had a week left and there was little he could do to change that.

Because we'd managed to get a fair amount of stuff done in Paris in pretty much a day, he'd wondered why I'd booked the place for four nights. If he'd had his way, we would have spent only two days in each city. When I was planning this trip, I thought that wouldn't be enough time to see everything worth seeing and really immerse ourselves in each place. As it turned out, Dad would've been happy with two hours in each city. Or however long it took for a hop-on/hop-off tourist bus to do a lap. He could just tick off the major tourist sites as we went past, sitting on the upper deck of the bus with two singlets under his shirt to avoid the cold.

Arriving in Caen, we checked in to our hotel, and for the first time on this trip we weren't sharing. It was a nice boutique hotel, containing only fifteen or so neat little rooms that had the feel of luxury about them, not just mass-produced furniture placed in the same configuration in room after room. Dad's and mine were a completely different layout. Heaven compared to the apartment in Paris.

Our time in Caen was like a holiday within a holiday. Separate rooms meant that for a few blessed hours, between sightseeing and dinner, we could get away from each other and sit in unfilled silence. Dad was free to talc all he wanted without complaint, and I was free to not answer strange questions or get lung cancer.

The countryside, away from the crowds, was a relief to Dad. Traffic was minimal and rather than a main thoroughfare our hotel was on a two-lane street, surrounded by cute two-storey attached terrace houses. We were on the outskirts (but not the horrible industrial outskirts) of the main part of Caen, so it felt like the suburbs – quiet and relaxed. I didn't dare take Dad out for a walk as all the surrounding streets were paved with cobblestones. Aside from visiting the D-Day beaches and going to some of the museums that would inevitably be attached to them, I had nothing solid planned. We'd be dropping back to the pace Dad had probably been expecting all along: one item of interest, followed by hours of nothing.

Dad didn't have an interest in World War II history like I did, but after the intense city life of Paris, going to a beach sounded alright to him, so that first afternoon we headed out to see the D-Day landing sites. We slowly drove from one beach to the next: Sword, Juno, Gold, Omaha and Utah. Our stays at each became shorter as we realised, after the first three, that they were all pretty similar. A bunker or two, a commemorative plaque here and there, and a museum. We didn't bother going into the first few, as I knew that Omaha Beach held the army cemetery, a host of museums and a theatre. By now I knew I couldn't use up all my Dad tickets too early, and didn't want to waste his limited attention span on a not-as-good museum.

We made our way through a few bunkers and over concrete embankments, constantly reminded of what occurred here by the uneven, pockmarked landscape, craters from the naval bombardment having grassed over in the seventy years since. We did visit the Arromanches 360, a cinema set up like a planetarium, replaying archive footage from the Battle of Normandy on the ceiling above us. The cinema was free for WWII veterans, which I thought was a nice gesture, though I wasn't sure how many of them would want to relive that time, and it did seem slightly cynical since as time went on fewer and fewer veterans would be around to take them up on the offer.

Then we arrived at Omaha, generally considered the main beach of the invasion, being the most heavily defended and where the Allies suffered the greatest casualties. This peninsula may have marked the beginnings of the Allies' counterattack on the Nazis, but for Dad it was a happy place, marking his own liberation from Paris.

We walked through the American army cemetery at Omaha Beach, a sea of white crosses that left me awestruck. Most of these deaths had occurred on the one day. It wasn't often I got to see the physical incarnation of sacrifice.

From here I wandered down to the beach in the hope of finding some memento, not really sure what I was expecting – perhaps a bullet casing, or an old rusted weapon. I wanted an item to bring back as a reminder of the trip that, unlike Dad's, didn't belong in a road. I wouldn't find it here.

Dad stayed up at the top of the cliffs as I walked down, his legs giving him way too much grief by this stage to even consider joining me in heading down the steep embankment. I didn't force the issue. I'd seen the problems Dad was having every time he got in and out of the car, and a walk down to the beach wouldn't have been pleasant for him.

On our leisurely drive back to the hotel, we soaked up the beautiful countryside, the roads dotted with tiny little not-even-towns. They had old houses set so close to the narrow, winding streets, I felt sure I was going to lose the bond on the hire car by tearing off a sideview mirror.

———

After some much-appreciated alone time, I headed over to Dad's room to work out what we'd do for dinner. We were both tired from being up early and walking the beaches, so trying to find somewhere to eat once again began to feel like a chore.

There was a restaurant attached to the hotel, and Dad asked, 'Why don't we eat here?'

It was a fair enough question, considering we could have jumped in the lift and been there in about 40 seconds. But the answer was: because I had looked at the menu earlier, and I knew him.

'We can . . . but it's a Michelin-starred restaurant.' I said.

'What's that?'

'It's a fancy degustation restaurant . . .' I responded, his blank look letting me know he didn't know what a degustation was. I kept going. 'You know, like eight courses —' Dad's eyes lit up, his mind completely misleading him, thinking of eight serves of any type of food.

I explained it was going to be small dishes of really fine, crafted food, something not in his repertoire. To Dad, fine, crafted food is a rolled-up slice of ham, perhaps with a tooth-pick through it. If there was some Coon cheese and a butter pickle at the end of the toothpick then it really was a formal occasion.

Experimenting was not high on Dad's list. He was in a 45-year eating groove and anything outside of that was not entertained. Dinner was ritually at 6 pm, unless some force of nature dictated otherwise. A polo shirt would cover him for pretty much any venue he wished to dine. And there was 'no need for the spicy food!' Mum told us kids that, before we were born, she managed to get him to throw caution to the wind and go to a Chinese restaurant – he ordered the mixed grill.

These days, Mum and Dad's dining experiences were generally bistro-based, complete with members' and seniors' nights, be they at the local pub or the footy club down the road. These places adhered to Dad's theory on food, which was that you should never be able to see plate. Every available space on the serving dish that could be covered with food should be covered with food. This was consistent with his suggested serving size of 'as big as your head'. If it happened to be bigger than your head that was a win, but certainly nothing smaller. He was probably upset that pizzas were round but came in square boxes, squandering potential deliciousness.

The Ivan Vautier restaurant we were about to dine in would have been awarded its Michelin stars for their 'high culinary merit'. They're rarely awarded extra stars because their foie gras and lobster marinated in Normandian pommeau is generously served in a bucket.

While Dad's eating habits made it appear as though he'd survived a famine during a depression, his cooking requirements were also 'no fuss'. Steaks were to be, 'Really well done, thanks.' When they arrived, the more burned the better – not that he could taste the charcoal outer, burying it under a tsunami of tomato sauce (from the pantry). The Eiffel Tower mightn't have been big enough, but if his chicken parma was an inch thick then you had his seal of approval and had given him a memory that would last a lifetime.

Like most families, growing up we had our weekly food routines. There was kai si ming, Mum's version of all-encompassing Asian, made up of beef mince, shredded cabbage and other assorted (read: leftover) veggies, with a mild spice flavouring that I imagined was a combination of curry powder and MSG.

We had chops, never steak. We weren't 'bloody millionaires'.

The only dish Dad would make was spaghetti bolognaise, his specialty. He used every available condiment and spice in the pantry, making the sauce thick, red and delicious. It also ruined the taste of a simple Napoli sauce for me – Dad's was so heavy and sweet that anything else was as worthless as eating a chip without salt.

Dad knew what he liked and stuck to it. We had our local pizza place, and there was never any thought of changing. Dad loved them and I'm sure thanks to his dedicated custom they came to love him too. When they answered the phone, the first thing they'd ask for was the address, to check if you were in their delivery zone. Upon hearing our address, they'd reel off our order before I had a chance to, starting with: family-sized capricciosa. That was for Dad. Alone. Family-sized. He'd eat that every Friday night after returning home from shopping with Mum.

Ours was a family of big serves. We ate it all, whether we felt like it or not. Countless times I'd sat at the table, my stomach stretched like an overinflated football, drifting into a coma, only for Dad to start light-heartedly cajoling me. 'Finish it. Come on, there's hardly any left.'

If I somehow managed to protest without bringing it all up again, he'd follow that up with, 'You're not wasting it!'

In Europe he'd so far gotten by without straying too far from what was familiar, sticking to the western, less cultured part of menus in restaurants and bakeries, which he could eat in large quantities.

But in Caen, emboldened, he said he was up for the Michelin dining experience even after I'd explained the concept to him. That made me excited too. Not so much for the food, although I was looking forward to that, but because I was enthusiastic about watching him during the meal. For that event I could have sold tickets for upwards of $5000 to anyone who knew him.

Michelin restaurants aren't known for their exceptional value, but I kept that part to myself. I wanted Dad to deal with the birdlike serves on their own merits, rather than calculating that he could have had six serves of the Windy Hill bistro's Friday night special fish and chips for the price of our first course.

The maître d' seated us at our table, the rest of the fairly small restaurant full with about eight couples. Even though it was a fairly nice establishment, the mood was relaxed and welcoming, Dad and I not feeling underdressed in our suitcase attire. Once we'd sat down we informed our waiter we'd be partaking in the degustation. I decided to order a glass of wine, expecting Dad to get a beer, when he suggested we should grab a bottle to share. I had never seen him drink wine. Ever. It was always beer.

He'd had a spirits cupboard when I was growing up, but it was stocked mostly with booze not recognisable to anyone. The cupboard had an Aldi feel to it, containing a Baileys knock-off called something like 'Cream of the Irish' and a whiskey probably called 'Gregfiddich'. The rest of the contents was padded out with undrinkably high-percentage homemade booze given to Dad by his customers.

As a teenager it was the worst cupboard to try and sneak a drink from. Not a Crème De Menthe in sight. How was I supposed to get tanked before a party? The only wine that was in the house was used for cooking, such was its value. As desperate as I was, I didn't dare go near the homemade stuff for fear of going blind.

I was happy to share a bottle of wine at Ivan Vautier, but let Dad know I was genuinely surprised. He informed me he used to drink it all the time. Dubious, I questioned him on which one, and he told me he was partial to a sparkling red called Cold Duck, to be precise.

He was describing a different person from the one I knew. If I'd walked into the house one day with a chilled sparkling red,

I'd have been mocked into oblivion. Not that it would be a one-way street; if I saw Dad drinking Cold Duck, I'd mock him incessantly too. Maybe that's why he stopped drinking Cold Duck, not wanting his children see him drinking something that sounds like it should be ingested by fourteen-year-olds in a park.

We ordered a nice bottle of sauvignon blanc from the Sancerre region of France, settling in to enjoy the most expensive drink we'd ever had together, shattering the previous record of 'Nine dollars for a beer!'

The degustation began with a shrimp mousseline, a combination of shrimp and mousseline.

Upon hearing shrimp, Dad naturally got excited. He loved Christmas because it meant prawns – Mum was not a fan of seafood, so prawns were off the menu the rest of the year.

Upon *seeing* shrimp mousseline, Dad became the opposite of excited. 'What is this?'

His look of utter bewilderment told me that serving him food in a tiny entree bowl was not going to cut it. It wouldn't have been the right thing to do, but I felt I should have gone into the kitchen to let the chefs know who they were dealing with.

'Everyone, that is Tom Rozenbachs out there. I don't think you realise who you're doing business with. That is a man who destroys a family-sized capricciosa every Friday night by himself. By. Him. Self. All of it. Don't serve him a meal in a bowl so tiny that if he was brought tartare sauce in it, he'd complain to the manager. And he's a man! He's expecting a knife that doubles as a jaws of life, not a flat, wide toothpick made for delicate eating, only good in the hands of a three-year-old with the dexterity of a surgeon. Lift your game! I want to see an improvement by the time dessert comes out. Or else you know a two-word review is coming your way.'

There are occasions in life when you know it'll be the last time you're doing something. The moment the first dish was served, Dad and I both knew this was one of those moments for him. I would have to savour every disappointed mouthful of fine dining that he took.

Any other time I'd be concerned Dad was too far out of his comfort zone, but I could afford to sit back and enjoy that dinner. The only danger was Dad passing out from malnourishment.

It was a night that would never be forgotten. Dad marvelled at the dishes, in his mind each more absurd and pointless than the last, from the sea scallop carpaccio to the Cévennes caramelised onions, which for Dad were disappointingly not sitting under a sausage in bread. Even as we headed into the seventh course, none of them was close to satiating his appetite. The night could only have been made better if, between the fourth and fifth courses, a jazz band came to play beside our table.

By the eighth and final course, I genuinely thought the kitchen were on to this disappointed foreigner. I imagined them hastily trying to create the most obscure dish they could, trying to rattle him one final time.

When it arrived, I felt I should stand and applaud: camembert ice-cream. Genius. All the coldness of ice-cream, with none of the taste of ice-cream. The look on Dad's face as he took his first bite went from delicious anticipation to shock to disgust within about a millisecond, his brain telling him in no uncertain terms that this wasn't right.

I photographed the moment, his face pure horror. He wasn't fearful, it was more as though he'd been the victim of a cruel prank, not unlike something he himself might do to an unsuspecting friend. 'Ah, good one – you said it would be ice-cream but instead it's a cheese that doesn't come conveniently sliced and wrapped in plastic. You got me. Now, where's the real ice-cream?'

Of course the waiter explained what each dish was as it was being served, but Dad never listened. He was probably too busy thinking about a steak so overcooked, every chef here would refuse to do it. I explained to him that it was camembert ice-cream. The two-word review finally came: 'That's shithouse.'

Then, for some reason, he continued eating. His contorted face told me he still wasn't enjoying it.

'What are you doing? I thought you hated it?' I asked, mystified.

'Not going to waste it – we bloody paid for it!'

I got up and ordered another bottle of wine, at the same time picking up the bill. Dad and I had been trying to outdo each other paying for dinners, but if he saw what they thought this dining experience was worth, we'd have to add on the price of a defibrillator. He and Mum once took cans of Coke with them to Hamilton Island in far north Queensland because they'd heard they were expensive up there.

Dad and I whiled away the evening with the wine that we both agreed was delicious, and he was at least able to enjoy the great selection of cheeses we had as dessert. I did have to give him some credit for being game enough to try this experience, even if he'd wound up hating it – I didn't imagine too many of the diners here would have been up for trying the Windy Hill bistro's schnitzel. Sure, Dad might have been misled by the idea of a big meal, but he was allowing himself to be nudged beyond his comfort zone.

Our Caen experience capped off with an awesome (for some) meal, the next day we headed back to Paris. Sitting at the main train station, Gare du Nord, amongst its vaulted roof and cheap eateries, waiting for the Eurostar train to take us to London, Dad broke the silence with yet another revelation: he was claustrophobic.

When we were planning the trip, I'd asked Dad if he was happy to get the train from Paris to London, through the Chunnel. He replied, 'Yes.' Stupidly, I took that to mean 'yes'.

I should have known it really meant, 'I'm claustrophobic and could think of nothing worse than being trapped in a tunnel underneath the English Channel, but I'll say nothing because to do so would be a sign of weakness.' So I guess we can all agree it was my own fault.

Who knows why he waited until that moment, after we'd already grabbed the Eurostar tickets, to tell me he was claustrophobic. He knew England wasn't a part of mainland Europe, that there was a body of water between the two. He would also have been aware it wasn't called the Channel Bridge, that the word 'tunnel' implied it was underground. Underground meaning enclosed. Enclosed meaning claustrophobia inducing.

For the thousandth time on this trip I wished he'd said something and allowed me to find another way. I wouldn't have cared; there were other options for getting to England. I had looked into getting the ferry from Calais, or we could have flown. Although after hearing about this fear I was glad I didn't go with my fourth option: locked in the back of a truck with refugees.

But admitting or showing fear had never been a thing in our house. When I was about eight, I overheard Mum and Dad telling some friends about a ghost they thought lived in our house. Mum recounted how she would be home alone and see something flash past in the hallway leading off the living room, only to find when she walked out to have a look that there was nothing there. Or at 2 am they'd both hear someone walking around the house – actual footsteps on the lino – and Dad would get up to tell us kids to go back to bed, only to discover we were all fast asleep.

Mum's a very spiritual person, so she was convinced it was the ghost of an elderly neighbour who had recently passed away in the house over the back fence. To get rid of the ghost, Mum held a séance, telling the spirit he was in the wrong house. She did this *BY HERSELF*. You know, just your casual afternoon séance. Scary movies freak me right out, but here's Mum just delving head first into the paranormal, calling out a ghost to leave the house. Which, based on movies I've seen, is a recipe for blood seeping out of the walls. All done before she casually got back into making dinner.

The sightings stopped after that.

I resolved never to eavesdrop again. I was eight. I didn't need to hear that. Not when our toilet was out the living room door, down a dark corridor at the back of the house, attached to the laundry, which opened up to the backyard. As everyone knows, the perfect way for ghosts to enter a house was from the backyard and through the laundry's flimsy sliding door. Trips to the toilet always ended with a five second burst of: flush—light switch off—bolt down dark corridor—explode through the door— casual stroll back into the living room as though I hadn't just sprinted for my life.

I don't remember either of my parents showing fear, or talking about the spectral sightings like they had been scared. Looking back, I can see they dealt with the situation as best they could. I probably would have just packed up everything I owned and moved to a deserted island, but each to their own.

Showing fear wasn't a thing in our family. There was never a spider incident that rendered someone paralysed. We just matter-of-factly trapped the spider with a glass, slid the paper underneath and took them outside. There was no throwing of shoes or other hysterics. I remember European wasps were high on the agenda every summer, Mum and Dad constantly reminding us to cover our cans of fizzy drink at all times, just in case one crawled in and we swallowed it when we had a drink. But we didn't walk around in bee-keeping outfits.

I'd love to say I was looking back at everything through rose-tinted glasses, but we were the type of family where, if someone lost their mind over something, they'd be reminded of it at every opportunity forever after. Anyone who ever entered our house knew about the time I lost it on the ferris wheel; I still don't think the Foxtel man needed to be told.

As we sped through the Chunnel, I tried to distract Dad from the darkness outside the train windows, asking him how long the claustrophobia had been a thing and why he'd never spoken about it. I didn't know if that was the right way to do it – to talk about the issue while he was experiencing it – but I figured it was better than letting him think about the walls slowly closing in and the fact the tunnel was probably only moments away from collapse because of all the water we were submerged under. In hindsight, I probably shouldn't have said that out loud either.

He didn't answer directly, instead deflecting by telling me he wouldn't have wanted to go into the catacombs in Paris, either. It had been on my list of potential sights, a series of tunnels underneath Paris filled with the bones of the dead to relieve the strain on the city's overflowing cemeteries. I'd been to catacombs in Lima and Peru and thought Dad might like to check it out. And as a metal-head, the stacks of bones looked like some of my favourite album covers. Dad kept his relief to himself when we discovered they were closed, because October is Europe's attraction-renovation season. Again, I said if he'd told me, I would've crossed it off the list.

I'd successfully distracted Dad from the Chunnel, but talking about the catacombs allowed him to make the claim that 'they suggest if you have gumboots with you, you put them on'.

As though you'd be out doing tourist things in Paris, decided to go into the catacombs, and just happened to have a pair of gumboots with you. 'Oh these? You think I should put them on? Well what do you know, after all those years of taking them out and never wearing them, they've finally paid off.'

Though at this stage of the trip I wouldn't have been surprised to find a pair of gumboots hidden in the east wing of Dad's suitcase.

For the rest of the train ride, my mind replayed all the places we'd been that were enclosed spaces. The crypt in the Bamberg cathedral, Paris's Metro system, the windowless bedrooms in our nightmare apartment. He seemed fine with it all, but now that I knew, I would actively try to avoid those situations. All it took was one actual, real conversation!

I made a note to cancel the 12-hour isolation tank session I had planned in London.

LONDON

As we stepped off the train at St Pancras in London, Dad loosened up almost instantly. He smiled, was chattier than he had been in days, and for the moment even seemed to be walking pain-free. The writing on all the signs was in English, the cars were on the right side of the road and, most importantly, it was not Paris. We could've pulled into Kabul Station and he'd have been happy.

There was also the sense that we were closer to the end of our journey than the beginning with only a week remaining, which gave us both something to look forward to.

It was my first time in London in a decade, not having visited since I unsuccessfully attempted to move there in 2001, giving up out of sheer misery. I arrived with high expectations, wanting to try to make it in stand-up in one of the world's hubs of comedy. But I was beaten down, arriving in the middle of winter with absolutely no idea of what to expect. I couldn't deal with the bleak conditions. Cold, overcast, wet, my tiny little mind blown by it getting dark at 3 pm. I slogged it out for two months before giving up, desperately missing home, depressed that a relationship had ended for this. Things weren't helped by the lack of smiles from the Brits in almost every facet of life. It seemed they were all as depressed by the gloominess as I was, and I longed for a happy stranger to come walking off an aerobridge smiling and talking to everyone.

Dad and I would be staying in Camden Town, which was easy enough to get to from St Pancras as it was only a few Tube stops away. Dad seemed fine with the prospect of going underground, though we'd have to navigate Friday night peak hour to get there. That would have been enough of a pain with standard luggage, but Dad's suitcase could easily have been attached to the back of the train and used as an extra carriage.

As we stepped onto the train, two guys in their mid-twenties saw us haul it on and immediately started ribbing Dad.

'Sure it's big enough, mate?'

'You got a body in there?'

'Is that your hotel room?'

Dad could not have loved this interaction any more if he'd tried. They were speaking English and they were giving him shit like people would back home. Dad had never been too serious about himself, always happy to have a laugh at his own expense. Whether it was his lack of tech know-how or being mocked by my mates for his homemade stick-man tattoo he did when he was fourteen, as long as it was good-natured he never minded.

It was the first time I'd seen him genuinely smile in over a week, and gave me confidence we'd finally found a place he might like.

The apartment in Camden Town was perfectly normal, which was another relief after Paris. Camden itself is a bit of an alternative area, with markets and a strong music scene. But it still has that London suburb vibe of tightly packed terrace houses surrounded by off-licences, betting establishments or chain pubs with names like the Slug & Lettuce, the Hungry Horse or the Soulless Rip-off.

As we left the apartment the next morning, I had high expectations. Dad seemed the most relaxed he'd been for the whole trip and London was going to have a higher hit rate of tourist attractions that he was aware of. He didn't even seem to mind that we had to walk to the next station down the line as Camden Town station was closed because the markets were on. Which Dad was happy to stroll through, looking at T-shirts of bands he'd never heard of, never intending to buy anything on offer. But at least he'd walked through them. London really had made him a new man.

I felt comfortable too; the two months I'd spent unemployed in London meant I knew where I was going, not having to stop every three seconds to make sure we were on the right track. I felt in a better place mentally for London this time around, perhaps because I knew what to expect, and, more importantly, when I was leaving.

We arrived at Embankment station, and as we exited up the escalators, our London adventures began. We walked out of the station to be met by the Thames and, on the opposite bank, the London Eye. My ferris wheel history and Dad's newly outed claustrophobia meant that we were never going to go for a ride on the Eye, so seeing it was enough for Dad.

He only had one thought about the giant wheel. 'Why isn't it on a park?'

It was an interesting question. The London Eye is located on the banks of the Thames and it's over one hundred metres high, so it offers excellent views stretching over greater London (I assume). But Dad seemed to think those views would be spoiled by the Thames, the river earning one of his brutal two-word reviews: 'It's dirty.' As though for some reason the people on the Eye would spend the whole time staring at the ground right below them.

I'm not sure what he was expecting; Melbourne's Yarra River is offensively brown all year round, so it's not as though he's used to glacial-blue rivers cutting through a city. He must have left his goggles and speedos in his mobile wardrobe, so I don't think he had plans to swim it, either. At least it didn't smell like cat piss.

Fortunately for Dad, a lot of London's tourist hotspots are in a big loop, fairly close to each other, so it was going to be an easy stroll to see most of them. We walked along the river to the iconic (to almost everyone but Dad) houses of parliament, Dad not taking it in as he was still distracted by the non-park Eye and filthy river.

Which brought us to Big Ben. Dad took it in for a bit, and then hit me with, 'Didn't think it'd be surrounded by buildings.' I took this to mean he thought the clock should somehow stand alone, maybe in a park. For a man who happily cut down any tree that got anywhere near his property, he suddenly seemed to have a real thing for parks.

He followed up with, 'Could've just looked at the Dimmeys clock.' Now, while that Richmond landmark is iconic to some of the people of Melbourne, it's barely a quarter of the size of Big Ben and it doesn't draw in millions of visitors from around the world. It's not like tourists get picked up from the airport and rush straight to Swan Street so they can witness for themselves this clocktower they've heard so much about (from Dad).

Then we were on to Buckingham Palace. Dad seemed fairly impressed by his first ever palace. Well, he wasn't actively *unimpressed*, so I took that as a victory. He was happy to stay for a while, most likely resting up, as we agreed that it's not a bad second home to have. His only gripe here was the same as pretty much every traveller: we couldn't get close to the place itself due to fences, security, beefeaters and selfie-sticks. Our photos would be taken from a distance. I imagined he mainly wanted to get closer so he could see if the Queen had the special hinges on her windows too.

As the typical heavy English drizzle set upon us, I decided walking wasn't on our agenda anymore as we'd end up drenched within the hour, so we jumped on the Tube to London Bridge station, with the intent of seeing Tower Bridge (the one most people assume is London Bridge). It was the first drawbridge Dad had seen in his life, and all he could think to ask was, 'Why's it that colour?'

The metal on the bridge was painted an inoffensive light blue, but perhaps his thinking was that bridges were grey and drab, and to paint them anything else was to misrepresent their bridginess. By then I'd given up trying to follow the logic of his needlessly articulated thoughts, so responded 'don't know' and left it at that. We walked on, and I pointed out the Tower of London, giving him a brief description based on recollections of my tour through it last time I was here: a historic castle where they tortured the absolute shit out of people with some amazingly sharp and pointy implements. That was more than enough information for Dad to forget the moment we walked on.

I'd organised for us to have dinner with my Spanish friend Lorenzo, a finance guru I'd met when he was living in Melbourne. He and his Australian wife, Sara, an opera singer, had since moved to London. Lorenzo was a good mate who I'd spent many a Sunday afternoon with, enjoying his homemade paella while Sara practised banging out a few arias in their bedroom upstairs.

If you've never been around opera singing, it's quite startling. It's not something that can be done at half volume. She punched it out at full blast, quite the change from the sounds of Triple R that normally permeated Brunswick.

Lorenzo chose a fancy-ish establishment in Belsize Park that had the menu of a very upmarket pub. Dad loved it, not least because this almost-fine-dining restaurant had steak. And not steak the size of your fingernail served on a hydroponically grown salt-cured pea. But an actual, life-sized steak.

I filled Lorenzo and Sara in with what was going on back home with the group of friends they'd left behind. I only had to fill in the occasional blank for Dad – he knew my friends well, so I didn't feel like talking about all of them left him out.

Dinner with other people was a good opportunity for me to hear what Dad thought about the trip. My fast walking came up far too often; apparently it was easier to tell complete strangers about the problem than me, his son, who was in a position to solve the problem. But he was effusive in his praise for the Autobahn, the workmanship of the cathedrals and beer for breakfast.

Then of course the inevitable came: Paris. I couldn't disagree with his appraisal of the apartment. It would have taken someone recently released from prison to think it was in any way habitable, and even then they'd probably commit a crime just to get back to the cleanliness of a cell. At least Dad had proved capable of laughing about it, so his subsequent trauma seemed under control. He mentioned again that the city smelled like cat piss, which amused Lorenzo and Sara. They'd clearly failed to pick that up during their trip the previous year.

Then Dad surprised me by saying everyone in Paris had been rude. I knew he'd not had the best time, but I didn't remember that part of it. I needed to know more.

'Who was rude?' I asked.

'Everyone.'

'When? Everyone was really helpful.'

I reminded him of the woman who, after I said 'catacombs' fifty times as slowly and with as little Australian accent as I possibly could, finally understood me enough to explain that they were closed for maintenance.

'Oh yeah,' he said.

'And what about the guy that helped us out of that car park?' I asked.

Again, Dad had to concede that a Parisian had helped us get out of trouble. I explained to Lorenzo and Sara that when we were leaving the car rental place to drive to Caen, our pass wouldn't let us out, stopping everyone from behind us from exiting as well. When I hit the intercom button the voice at the other end only spoke French, leaving us in yet another incoherent stand-off. Then the guy behind us exited his car, asked what was happening and explained the situation to the guy on the intercom. The boom gate went up, we said thank you to this kind stranger, and were on our way. It couldn't have been a more pleasant experience.

I dislike rudeness as much as the next person, but I couldn't let Dad re-write history for the sake of hating Paris. I made a note to double-check with Mum what he told her upon our return, in case he created a story about us almost getting robbed but only being saved by the gaffer tape in his suitcase.

As we were served our dinner (Dad finally getting his well-done steak, which meant all our meals were delayed), he recounted with joy the afternoon tea in the suburbs of Munich that was basically conducted in the dark, and he talked Lorenzo and Sara through the Michelin-starred degustation, of course including the camembert ice-cream.

It was good to get some live feedback on how the trip had gone, and it gave me a sense that I hadn't done such a bad job after all. During the last two weeks I'd felt like I had been making Dad do most things against his will, but it seemed he'd appreciated the sights and scenes of Europe at some level.

Though there'd been some tense moments, Dad seemed to be looking back at most of what we'd done with good humour and fondness. I mentally patted myself on the back, knowing I'd been vindicated in incessantly pressuring him into doing things he didn't want to do.

Usually it's the role of the parent to be firm with their kids, forcing them do something for their own good. Certainly that's the way it had been for me. For so much of this trip the roles had been reversed, as time and again it fell to me to be the bad guy, forcing Dad to do all these things he was now joyfully recounting.

Despite my babysitting difficulties, I'd always liked to think I would be a fun dad rather than strict with my kids. I guess every parent thinks that at the beginning. Everyone starts out assuring themselves that they won't be like their own parents, just taking things in their stride, unruffled, until they realise it's kind of hard to retain a carefree sense of joy when someone is mashing playdough into the carpet.

I knew Uncle Adam was definitely fun. I'd swan in for a few hours, muck around, crack some gags, make some kids laugh, then walk away leaving behind me whatever mess I'd created. Be it sugar-based hyperactivity or accidentally teaching them inappropriate language (they'd learn it eventually anyway), I was carefree.

I never wanted to be the cause of trauma, but that did happen when I visited my friend Dave one Christmas. His son, Rafferty, had been given a trampoline, telling me it was from Santa. I was happy to live with this lie.

'Daddy, Daddy, can Adam come on the trampoline with me?' Raff asked Dave.

'Yeah, if he wants to, of course he can,' Dave replied. He looked at me to say, 'You don't have to but you'll be letting a three-year-old down if you don't.' I knew that look well.

Rafferty climbed in and I followed, Dave zipping us in from the outside. I should have known right then that it wasn't going to end well. Raff was from a different generation – a generation that had trampolines with nets around them, designed to keep children safe.

But life isn't always safe. Old trampolines were a metaphor for life: if you got too close to the edge, if you tried too hard and got a bit ahead of yourself, life was going to give you a lesson. Everyone over thirty reading this learned as a child that gravity and faces don't mix. My sister Michelle bounced herself off our neighbour's trampoline and ended up faceplanting into the springs. She's now one of the most conservative people I know, and I put it down to that experience.

Before I go on, I should point out Rafferty was a first-born. He didn't have an older brother to torment him and teach him unwelcome life lessons. Like that a fist may strike your face at any moment. I'll forever be in Jason's debt for teaching me that one.

As we played around, Rafferty fell over. Not a big deal. Happens hundreds of times on a trampoline. Perhaps someone had given him a nudge, but with no CCTV cameras, there was simply no way to know for sure.

Now, what's the one thing you should do when someone has fallen over on a trampoline?

[Pause while reader says, 'DOUBLE BOUNCE!']

That's right, you double bounce them.

I found out the hard way you didn't do that to a three-year-old. In my mind I figured if he'd been on a trampoline before, then he'd been double bounced. It's a rite of passage.

Instead I discovered that hysterical laughter sounds exceptionally similar to hysterical crying. It took way too long for me to recognise those weren't a snot bubble and urine stain of joy. If you've ever wanted to feel like an arsehole, or a bully, or an arsehole bully, then having a screaming child waiting for you to unzip a net so they can be released from your torment is a sure-fire recipe.

An activity that only minutes earlier was so much fun had suddenly turned into a torture session for Raff. I could still hear his sobs in the house as I climbed from the trampoline, shaking my head and letting out a sigh as a sign of apology to Dave.

Uncle Adam may not have always got it right, but Son Adam was on the right path. Buoyed by Dad's storytelling at dinner the night before, for our next day in London I thought a fun excursion (I was starting to feel like a teacher dragging around an uninterested Year 8 kid) would be to visit Harrods, the luxury department store. I knew Dad would be aware of it, not least because of Mum's love for Princess Di. Mum was devastated when she died, and wanted vast photo coverage of Buckingham Palace and anything else royal related we might stumble across. Harrods would also be a change of pace from seeing something historical or educational.

And being modern, it would have escalators, which if we rode them properly would only have Dad counting to 'one'.

We wandered the various departments of Harrods, surrounded by incredible luxury and wealth. Dad was just as blown away as in the duty-free store, this time marvelling at how expensive things he wouldn't normally buy could be. He was completely in his element with so many price tags to inspect and comment on.

'You should get Mum one of those tote bags. She'd love it,' I suggested, pointing out a Harrods bag.

Dad looked at it for a second. 'How much is thirty pounds?'

I did a quick calculation. 'I don't know, about fifty bucks.'

'I'm not paying fifty dollars for a bag. Fifty dollars! For a bag!'

You'd think I had suggested he spend his money on a £900 Givenchy handbag. I argued that the tote bag wasn't about the value for money, that he could afford it and that Mum would have really liked it. None of those arguments helped. He couldn't justify spending that much money on a tote bag. And that was that.

It wasn't until later that I thought perhaps I could have bought Mum the bag myself. But I figured I'd already given her the gift of getting Dad out of her hair for three weeks. Nothing in all of Harrods was as valuable as that.

After keeping our budget on track in Harrods, we spent the day roaming inner London as we had in the Tiergarten, with no destination. I hoped Dad wasn't getting too attached to our strolls, because it certainly wasn't going to happen when we got back to Melbourne.

We wandered around, the pace slow, as I pointed out Carnaby Street, Soho, Piccadilly Circus, Covent Garden, Leicester Square, Hyde Park, Trafalgar Square and more. Places he'd not be able to recount if his life depended on it. He saw them all.

Though Dad walked around without much complaint, I could see he was bored. If he wanted to walk around aimlessly, he could do that back home with Mum every Friday night at the Airport West Westfield. He didn't need to be 17 000 kilometres away from home to do it.

We still had three more days in London and the tourist attraction tank was running low. I knew I'd have to really sell anything more I wanted Dad to do and spread things out to cover the remaining days. But I felt I had his trust, now that he'd had his first opportunity to regale people with tales about his trip to Europe. Whether he enjoyed it or not, on reflection he could see that everything we'd done had served a purpose: he had travel stories. Now it would be his turn to be the most annoying and boring person at a dinner party.

Over the last two weeks I'd also adapted the way I went about things. I'd learned to lower my expectations, to not expect Dad to be amazed by anything at all, and not to overload him with too many things in one day. I still pushed him, knowing he wouldn't do anything if I didn't get him out of his comfort zone, but we'd finally found a balance.

———

That balance included having more downtime in our accommodation. That evening in London, as I was reading my book, relaxing in our apartment, I heard Dad fiddling with the front door. Having moved on from the windows of Europe, he'd noticed a unique mechanism on that lock.

Again it was handle related. To paraphrase (read: I didn't really listen to what Dad said), if you turned the handle down it opened like a normal door; if you turned it up it would semi-lock the door, only openable from the inside. 'But still locked from the outside, Adam.' If you turned the lock after that, it would lock the door from both inside and out.

It didn't matter to me. I was inside, reading my book, happy he was playing with the lock and not annoying me by announcing the water pressure. For those who care, London had great water pressure. I'll leave you to imagine what Paris's water pressure had been like.

I managed about four pages of distracted reading while he was going CLICK, HANDLE TURN, CLICK CLICK, DOOR OPEN, DOOR CLOSE, HANDLE TURN, CLICK CLICK, DOOR OPEN, DOOR CLOSE, KNOCK KNOCK KNOCK KNOCK.

He'd locked himself out. I stood and put the book down, but paused, considering leaving the door shut, before going over and letting him in.

'That's a great lock.'

I responded, 'That's good.'

Now that Dad was back inside, I suggested a few things for us to do the next day. I knew they weren't high on his list (i.e. he'd never heard of them), but we'd been to all the main sites and I was forced to offer up lesser-known ones. In my mind they were no less interesting, but I knew it was going to take something special on my part to get them over the line.

The Churchill War Rooms, Shakespeare's Globe Theatre, Lord's cricket ground – all were knocked back. I was so desperate I threw in the Tate Modern gallery, of course to no avail. I knew I'd reached the edge of my sanity when I suggested Madame Tussauds, even though I could think of nothing worse than looking at famous candles-in-waiting. Again, a resounding 'no'.

I was proud of the level of patience I'd shown throughout the trip. I'd never been a patient person – people generally annoyed the hell out of me. But this time was different. I had a purpose. I was doing the trip for Dad. I wanted to say thanks for everything he had done for me throughout my life, and part of that was keeping my cool when I normally wouldn't.

Life wasn't built for people to get along every second of every day. Overseas trips are worse, small annoyances heightened by the stress and expectation of travel, plus the close quarters, tension building like the single drops of water on the forehead of a torture victim.

DRIP. Reminding Dad to get his Oyster travel card out every time we entered or exited a train station.

DRIP. When we were at the pub watching the soccer, and I asked, 'Are you hungry?' and he replied, 'Yes and no.'

DRIP. Taking his Oyster pass from him and holding onto it for him, only handing it to him when he needed to use it, like you would for a child.

DRIP. Drowning his fish and chips in tartare sauce because, 'I paid for it. Not giving it back.'

DRIP. 'I probably should've worn these shoes in.'

I had never been in a proper argument with Dad. There was the occasional shouting match when I was younger, but that's how we dealt with things in my childhood. There were no rational conversations to work things through. It went from nothing to shouting to over, like a summer storm. Though we both knew that living under his roof meant I could only push disagreements so far, anyway.

The most heated discussion we ever had was after I'd moved back home when comedy hadn't bred instant success. I wasn't really paying my way around the house. Dad had had enough, I dug my heels in, and luckily Mum was there to calm things down, sending us our separate ways before things got out of hand.

But Mum wasn't here now. Every person has their limits, and after two and a half weeks of struggle, Dad relentlessly shutting down my suggestions had taken its toll. The dam wall burst.

'Jesus, Dad, can you help me out here? I'm suggesting all this stuff and all you do is knock it back. You're really starting to piss me off!'

Turned out Dad had his own dam, which had also been at bursting point.

'I don't want to do any of that! Maybe I'll just go home tomorrow.'

I was ready to fire back, about to ask him exactly how he was going to organise that without me, when he cut me off. 'I didn't even want to do this stupid trip anyway.'

Dad = straw. Me = camel. My back = broken.

I lost it. I spoke to him in a way I never thought I would, or could. To anyone, let alone my dad. It was anger, it was hatred, it was pain. If there was such a thing as an eight-barrel shotgun (a double, double, double, double), I gave it to him with all eight barrels.

'Are you fucking serious? *YOU* didn't want to do this trip? The only reason I'm here is for you. I'd rather be overseas with my friends, not wasting my fucking time with you. This is bullshit! Fuck you! I am out of here!'

And before I did something stupid, like throw a punch or burst into tears, I stormed out.

Except Dad had locked the door. And I couldn't work out how to open it. I stood in front of it twisting knobs, yanking handles, kicking at it, muttering to myself, 'How does this fucking stupid fuck —'

All the while Dad stood behind me, giving me instructions, 'Turn it that way. No, *that* way.'

Eventually I managed to open the door and leave the

apartment, having completed the single worst storm-out humanity had ever known.

I stood in the street, adrenaline pumping through my veins, shaking as though I'd had too much cough medicine. I didn't know what to do. This was as furious as I'd ever been with Dad.

My first thought was to walk back into the apartment, throwing in a few extra reasons why I was there in the first place and where I'd rather be. But I knew that wasn't going to help. I'd said my piece, and though a thousand thoughts bounced around my head, none of them particularly nice, there was no point in piling more on.

I didn't contemplate going straight back in to apologise either, as that would have been viewed as a sign of weakness. I couldn't have risked that.

I walked through Camden absentmindedly, swearing and muttering to myself like the sufferer of either an unchecked mental illness or the debilitating effects of travelling with a parent. Because it was London, I found myself outside a pub within a hundred metres, as good a place as any to gather my thoughts. And seriously dull the pain.

Backing down from a fight had always been one of the hardest things for me to do. Firstly, I always think I'm right – I rarely shout in agreement. Mostly, though, I didn't do it because backing down is not something that happened in my family, since we didn't really fight in the first place. There had been shouting, but that would just be at us kids for not doing stuff: setting the table, taking the dog for a walk, homework. Nothing serious.

I'd only ever heard Mum swear at Dad once, calling him a 'shithead'. I was stopped in my tracks, thinking, 'Whoa, that is serious! He must've really done something wrong here.' Mum swearing was cool, but I never found out the source of the trouble, as I knew to keep moving lest I cop some fire from her as well.

We didn't talk about things. We'd always been an 'actions, not words' type of family. Saying 'I love you' was like putting sauce in the fridge – it simply wasn't the done thing. It felt weird to even consider it. Maybe someone tried saying 'I love you' once, but like the sauce, it would have been shut down pretty quickly.

If there was ever any conflict, whatever happened at the flash-point was the final outcome and the disagreement was never spoken of again. That didn't mean it was the end of things and I'd move on; to the contrary, I continued to dwell on whatever it was. But those feelings were pushed deep inside, and no one ever had to suffer the indignity of admitting they'd been wrong. It was just the way our family rolled.

As I ordered my third pint, I knew that had to change. If I went back in and pretended nothing had happened then we wouldn't have solved anything. All it would do was plant the seed for a lifelong grudge between Dad and me. A grudge that would grow to the size of an oak tree by the time we got back to Australia.

Pretending nothing was wrong would also ensure that every time I thought about the fight in the future I'd become more and more bitter, knowing I'd held my tongue against my better judgement. It was now or never.

I felt sick as I approached the apartment, every possible scenario running through my head. Not one of them involved Dad saying sorry. Even in my fictions he was unrelenting. In my head he'd just sat down to watch TV the moment I'd walked out.

I knew what I said to him would have to be a balancing act. I had to be articulate, stay calm and not get sucked into raising my voice.

When I opened the surprisingly unlocked door, I found Dad sitting the couch. The TV wasn't on. Perhaps he'd been thinking about it too. Or maybe he was still marvelling at the lock. It was hard to tell.

I apologised first. I explained my frustration at getting every one of my suggestions shot down without any consideration of the effort I'd put into them. I said I had tried really hard to make our trip enjoyable for him, and that it would be appreciated if he tried to help me. I wasn't asking for him to suddenly lead a tour through the Imperial War Museum, but to at least try some of my ideas. Or consider them for at least ten seconds before knocking them back. I also reminded him that he'd agreed to the trip and wasn't there under duress.

The flood gates open, I kept going, telling him that finding out he didn't want to do the trip really hurt. I said I'd given up my time for this – for him – and I just wished he'd show some appreciation. I hadn't wanted to say, 'Hey, I hope you appreciate me doing this favour for you,' because it was his example that had set me on a path in life where I considered actions to be stronger than words. But it seemed he wasn't picking up on my actions, so I had to resort to words.

Dad apologised too. 'Okay.'

Being fluent in Tommy Rozenbachs, I translated this as, 'You're right, I have been hard work on this trip. I'll try harder to appreciate what a wonderful son you are. Thanks for being here, and this really does show me how much you love me and your gratitude for what I did for you growing up.'

That was the last conversation we ever had about that fight. Until then we'd been two bulls in a paddock, ready to butt heads, but we'd avoided further confrontation. I guess it might even be described as a nice moment.

Even though I felt like I was enabling him to be a quitter, I told him I'd look into getting us on an earlier flight home. He seemed pleased with that, even though we were giving up a marathon just as we'd spotted the finishing line. He wanted to go home, and I knew if we stayed any longer it would just end up causing me more frustration. Packing it in early was win–win.

I told him I'd get onto changing the flights as soon as possible, but nothing could be guaranteed. In the meantime, I suggested we should head back out, grab a beer and try to find something of interest to him for us to do the next day.

'Come on,' I said as we headed outside. 'Let's go yell at some cobblestones.'

As we walked to the pub, Dad brought up a topic from the day before, which let me know he had at least partially taken in what I'd said.

'Why don't we do that Frankenstein walking tour?'

For a split second I had no idea what he was talking about. Then I remembered to think like Tommy. 'You mean Jack the Ripper?'

'Same thing.'

I was proud of myself. I'd handled this extremely delicate situation with diplomacy I didn't realise I had, which in turn made me feel like I was ready for fatherhood. I'd neither lost nor killed Dad, two fairly high prerequisites for becoming a parent (I assume).

I had even grown as a person in those three weeks, having found an inner peace I never knew existed. Before we left, I was the most impatient person you could ever meet. Supermarkets, cafes, roads; they'd all felt the wrath of my impatience. If someone missed the green arrow at a set of traffic lights, I'd be banging on their window, screaming, 'You dickhead, you missed the arrow, what is wrong with you?!?!' And that was just as a pedestrian.

As we made our way through Europe, avoiding a Dad-induced aneurysm every five minutes led me to a level of zen I hadn't known was possible. Just like Dad teaching me to drive with incessant noise had made me a far better driver, three weeks of his insanity made me a calmer, better, more responsible person.

He did it. THE SON OF A BITCH DID IT.

We woke to the fortunate news we'd been moved to an earlier flight and that we'd be leaving that night. We didn't make it the full twenty-one days I'd planned for us, but for the sake of our relationship, this was the better outcome.

Dad had a spring in his step, happy to take to the London streets one very last time. He'd be home soon.

We had lunch with Lorenzo at the 700-year-old Leadenhall Market in the financial district, a beautiful undercover market with an ornate roof. Dad added Spanish food to his list of things he'd never tried before, Lorenzo having taken us to a restaurant of his home country's cuisine. Initially Dad didn't think the serves of tapas were big enough, but in the end we managed to order enough of them to satisfy his hunger.

At the end of lunch I said goodbye to Lorenzo, and he laughingly wished us luck for the very short remainder of our journey. We both knew he wasn't really joking.

With only a few hours to kill, our last London moments were spent walking around Covent Garden Market. It could have been anywhere, neither of us really paying attention to our surroundings, both just killing time until we were on that flight home. I could see Dad was tired, and I knew by this stage there was no point asking him how he was.

'We should head back so we can pack and then head out to the airport. What do you reckon?' I asked, pretending to give him an option.

'No worries,' he replied.

As we headed into Covent Garden Tube station, I'd forgotten it didn't have escalators, so felt bad for making Dad trudge down one last set of steps. He was silent, and I figured this was the last thing he needed, but at least that would be it. He could relax at the airport and on the plane.

As we reached the platform I could see our train was already there. Reluctantly I said, 'Sorry, Tommy, we've got to get on this train.'

We both bolted, Dad putting in one last effort to ensure we made it. We stood in the carriage, both getting our breath back, and after about fifteen seconds Dad leaned in and said, 'Two hundred and five.'

MELBOURNE

It was night-time when we landed in Australia. We both felt better than we did after the flight to Europe, mainly because I'd convinced Dad he should try business class at least once in his life. 'You can recline the seats like a bed' was all it took to get him to agree, happy to shell out his hard-earned to be able to turn left upon boarding rather than right into economy. But no way he'd pay $50 for a Harrods tote bag for Mum. Overall he thought business class was okay, mainly because in both London and Bangkok we got to sit in a comfortable airport lounge with a buffet and free drinks. Well worth the extra cash.

As we taxied to the terminal in Melbourne, I sat in silence, reflecting on the journey in its entirety. Now that we were finally home and the trip was consigned to history, I felt that I'd climbed my Everest. I'd learned about my dad, my family, I'd kept my cool (mostly) in the most trying of circumstances and now we had things to bond over that no one else in the family would have.

As clichéd as it was, the trip had brought us closer together.

My thoughts were interrupted when Dad asked, 'Will you be staying at our place tonight?'

I lived fifteen minutes from their place. 'Nah, think I'll be right. Thanks though.'

The trip hadn't brought us *that* close.

It seemed fitting that Dad's suitcase was the last out on the carousel. As the baggage-claim area cleared, we stood by, me with my bag, waiting for Dad's. I presumed it was being used to temporarily chock the plane's wheels.

Once it came out we cleared customs without me having to tell him to get his passport ready and headed home to a hero's return. Mum, Michelle, Jason and his fiancée Claire were all there, wanting to hear about the trip and how much of my sanity I'd retained.

Dad proudly showed off his Parisian cobblestone, ignoring my sister's, 'What did you bring that home for?'

He was stunned to find out that the card we'd sent to Mum from Munich never arrived. To this day he still doesn't understand how that happened. 'You saw me, I wrote the right address and we had more than enough stamps. More than enough.'

'What did you bring back?' Mum asked me.

I held up Dad's boarding pass from our flight home.

'This. This is going to be my daily reminder of what I went through.' Mum shook her head, but I'd planned to put it on the desk in my office, and whenever I'd get frustrated about something I could look it and think, 'You can get through anything.'

PARIS AND OTHER DISAPPOINTMENTS

Now that he was a seasoned traveller, Dad was asked where he'd go next.

'I'd like to see India,' he said.

'India?' I butted in. 'You thought Paris stank! You think you could handle the slums of Mumbai?'

'I'd only go for two days.'

No way was I putting my hand up for that trip, not even for two days.

My time with Dad had given me a new appreciation for Mum, and I took her aside to tell her I thought she was a saint for putting up with him. I could hardly imagine forty years of what I'd just been through. I was genuinely touched to have a new perspective on how much they really did love and care for each other, which would form the basis of the application when I nominated Mum for Australian of the Year.

Jason asked Dad what his favourite part of the trip was. After a pause, he answered, 'I'd have to say sitting on the plane and hearing, "We've been in the air for five hours, and we're still in Australia." And I thought: what a bloody place.'

Three weeks in some of Europe's most remarkable cities, seeing ancient and extraordinary landmarks, witnessing the remnants of turning points in world history, reconnecting with his birthplace and discovering extended family we'd thought lost. Three weeks of torturous indecision, endless frustration and pointless questions. For that.

ACKNOWLEDGEMENTS

To all at Penguin Random House for their help and dedication – Jake, for putting me in touch with the right people, Cate for taking a chance on me, and Nikki and Sophie for coming to the rescue. To my editor, Johannes, thank you. You know your stuff, and knew how not to get in the way of the comedy. Alex, amazing job with the cover. Could not be happier.

Stef, thanks for being so supportive, from stand-up show all the way through to the book. It means a lot.

Rachel and Jill, your authoring knowledge and experience helped me through the rough [read: writer's block] patches. Was good to know I wasn't the first author to hate the process.

Ellen, thanks for taking the time out to read the bits I was struggling with and telling me it was funny and conveyed what I wanted it to.

Soph, thanks for listening. And talking me off a ledge week after week. You were so great with your feedback. And can't thank you enough for the help with the cover. We nailed it.

Kitty, you're a superstar for reading an entire first draft! Your feedback was invaluable. Can't thank you enough. Hope this is in a big enough font for you to read.

Dad, massive kudos for being such a good sport. I know I was annoying too (probably), so I appreciate you putting up with me. You never asked to be the star of a show and now a book, but you've done it all with great humour. Thanks Tommy.

Mum. Thanks for instilling in me a love of books; finally you get to read one by me. Also: you really are a saint. I don't know how you do it.

Love you both. There, I said it.

And finally, to Maurice Koechlin, Émile Nouguier and Stephen Sauvestre for designing the Eiffel Tower, which, although generally loved by most of the world, would be looked upon with disdain some 123 years later. I really couldn't have done this without you.